Save the Date

You are Invited

Books by Wesley B Raphael Sr

A Crying Shame

Beyond Destiny

Converting the Soul

Finding Grace Beyond Destiny

Save the Date

Save the Date

You are Invited

By Wesley B Raphael Sr

A Thoughts of Peace Publication

Printed in the United States of America

ISBN: 978-1-387-98430-5

Copyright ©2022 by Wesley B Raphael Sr.

Published by Thoughts Of Peace Publications aka Wesley B Raphael Sr

A Thoughts of Peace Publication

This book was made possible through Lulu.com on-demand publishing tools

Lulu Enterprises, Inc.
3131 RDU Center, Suite 210
Morrisville, NC 27560
919-459-5858

The Marketplace for
Diaital Content

Cover layout and design by Wesley B Raphael, Sr.

Cover art and illustrations are created from Microsoft Office Stock images 2020.

Bible Translations* used:

New Living Translation NLT

God's Word GW

King James Version KJV**

New International Version NIV

Easy Reading Version ERV

English Standard Version ESV

*No Paraphrased Bibles are quoted in this book
**Default King James Version used when not cited

TABLE OF CONTENTS

WHAT IS THIS BOOK?

Save the Date is a special invitation or re-invite to spend some quality time with God. This invitation is a Revelation of Jesus Christ. It is an important message to show God's great passion for you which he revealed from the very beginning when he established the Sabbath Day.

It is my desire that you will see Jesus Christ in a way that you may have never seen him before as Lord of the Sabbath and as such my hope is to share with you the important truths about the Sabbath that we have forgotten or did not notice.

We have all sinned and we have all failed to ease our own burdens and pains. Despite our efforts, we have not conquered death. We have nothing that we can do to remove our guilt, sin and shame. Christ says, *"Come to me, all you who are weary and burdened, and I will give you rest."* Matthew 11:28.

With Christ's Disciples being accused and legally guilty of breaking the Sabbath, Christ's response challenges Sabbatarians and those who are ignorant of the Sabbath by declaring his mission and purpose as well as defining his ultimate authority: He declared what God desires: *"If you had known what these words mean, 'I desire mercy, not sacrifice,' you would not have condemned the innocent."* Matthew 12:7 NIV

Christ declared them innocent making it clear that his mission was about clearing guilt and forgiving sins. His

1

mission was a mission of Mercy and Grace ordained from the very beginning. His great authority in these matters is implied in his connection to the Sabbath. Christ made very clear, the Sabbath's importance to all mankind. The Sabbath connects us to Christ's Mission on our behalf and Christ declared who he truly was:

"For the Son of Man is Lord of the Sabbath"
Matthew 12:8 NIV

Christ invites us to seek to know and understand his Sabbath. This book is an open invitation from Christ for you to learn and relearn about what the Sabbath really is and for whom it is.

Then he said to them, "The Sabbath was made for man, not man for the Sabbath. *Mar 2:27 NIV*

These verses turn our focus back toward Jesus and his Loving Father who sent him. The Sabbath is very special and holds a real connection to the Marriage Supper of the Lamb reference in Revelations. Christ compare the Kingdom of Heaven to a Marriage or great Wedding occasion for which an invitation was made. It weekly reminds us of the great plans God has for us. Promising something beyond our imagination.

That is what the Scriptures mean when they say, "No eye has seen, no ear has heard, and no mind has imagined what God has prepared for those who love him." *1 Corinthians 2:9 NLT*

Despite the abundance of access to information, many of us, have not really taken advantage of that access. Today information accuracy has also become trivialized by the lazy assumption that all sources are equal, and that ease of access is the same as reliability.

Information we once searched diligently for was a foundation of education and knowledge building. Like lazy students, we seek crib notes, summaries, and soundbites. Today's culture is more comfortable with snippets of information, media blurbs and tabloid headlines with misleading provocative images, even memes.

We don't get the whole story and many times we do not get the truth. Perhaps, we do not even want the whole story, facts, or truth. As long as it does not offend us or require much research, we are willing to tolerate ambiguity and uncertainty until the lack of information proves dangerous which is often too late. It is all just as the Bible predicted.

"For the time will come when they will not endure sound doctrine; but after their own lusts shall they heap to themselves teachers, having itching ears; And they shall turn away their ears from the truth, and shall be turned unto fables." 2 Timothy 4:3-4

No one seems to want detailed explanations and yet we often reject the simple ones.

For example: A truly short profession such as "God is Love" is quickly debated and often challenged without even a desire to know the truth. Fortunately, God has no problem proving himself. It is us who have the problem taking the time to listen, study and believe. Are you willing to study? I want to show you how you just how much God really loves you.

Perhaps you have never received or perceived this testimony of God's love that I will be sharing with you. Perhaps you have only heard of the Sabbath or have accepted it only from a logical and legal sense then you need to read further.

I am guilty of having a knowledge of God without making the effort of truly seeking him. I am ashamed to admit it because as a result I have played the hypocrite, misrepresenting knowledge of the Godhead: God the father, God the son and God the Holy Ghost.

I was claiming to be a Christian while living a life of selfish ignorance of the very God whose name I have boldly claimed and professed for years. Nevertheless, I thank God for his unmatched Grace. He has given me a mission and a purpose to tell the world about his love.

CHAPTER 1

GOD'S PLAN

Jesus shouted to the crowds, "If you trust me, you are trusting not only me, but also God who sent me. For when you see me, you are seeing the one who sent me. I have come as a light to shine in this dark world, so that all who put their trust in me will no longer remain in the dark. I will not judge those who hear me but don't obey me, for I have come to save the world and not to judge it.

But all who reject me and my message will be judged on the day of judgment by the truth I have spoken. I don't speak on my own authority. The Father who sent me has commanded me what to say and how to say it. And I know his commands lead to eternal life; so I say whatever the Father tells me to say." John 12:44-50 NLT

I have been baptized not once but twice, not because my baptism was incomplete the first time but because of my chronic disobedience, It was an outward result of my personal unbelief and doubt.

When I finally dared to open God's word and allowed him to speak to me during personal Bible study and hearing of the word, I came face to face of what God's Grace truly is. I wanted to know how I should and how I can respond to it. I am believing you would like to know as well.

Please do not turn down this opportunity because it will prove to be a priceless truth. It will be life changing and character altering because we cannot just know Jesus without becoming like him. His invitation is to eternal life.

We owe our existence to God. How can we claim to understand our existence let alone the existence of God? It is a personal question and a core question of many philosophy students. What is the purpose of our existence? In fact, this question is not limited to secular concerns and is a core of Biblical Theology which begins with the genesis of our existence.

I know you have questions. Have you ever wondered if there is anything after this life? Have you been fearful of God's judgement? Perhaps you are confused believing that somehow you can please God while trying to follow the instructions of individuals whom you may think are holier than you? In your heart of hearts, can you ever see that actually happening?

How can you know God by simply following the advice of those who are as sinful as you? You may know more about them that causes you to doubt the importance of the very God they profess to know and love. This can be very confusing and discouraging at the same time.

I only ask for your patience and prayerful curiosity. Perhaps God has prepared you to receive answers in your search for answers to the questions that you have been plagued with for so long.

Knowing how flighty we can be in our secular and our spiritual lives you may ask yourself how God could be so loving, given your own short comings? We often fall short of the expectation and results that we had hoped to achieve.

The feeling of being stuck is very real for believers and unbelievers. It is time to get unstuck even when our efforts and labors seem to increase while our results continually diminish. God is speaking to you today.

"Come, all you who are thirsty, come to the waters; and you who have no money, come, buy and eat! Come, buy wine and milk without money and without cost. Why spend money on what is not bread, and your labor on what does not satisfy? Listen, listen to me, and eat what is good, and you will delight in the richest of fare." Isaiah 55:1-2 NIV

I want you to think about worship as it relates to your relationship with God. How do you even worship God? Do you understand why you should? Perhaps you have wondered if worship even matters. Perhaps you are struggling with the questions of how you should worship, when and where you should worship?

What are you getting from your worship? Has your worship experience become like a blind date, full of possibilities, questions and anxiety and mostly ending in disappointment? This confusion must end starting now.

God is not confused about our origins and God has provided a way for us to find our groundings and reset our faith. Many have heard about faith and have tried to master and tame it, but faiths potential remains with God who gave it to us.

"Faith shows the reality of what we hope for; it is the evidence of things we cannot see." Hebrews 11:1 NLT

There is a reality that we all share, and that reality is that our very existence is purposeful, and our purpose can be found and understood. It is the belief that our lives can and should be meaningful and not meaningless. That reality causes us to seek our purpose for if we sincerely seek the truth, we will find it. It's all apart of God's plan

"Ask and it will be given to you; seek and you will find; knock and the door will be opened to you. For everyone who asks receives; the one who seeks finds; and to the one who knocks, the door will be opened." Matthew 7:7-8

CHAPTER 2

AFFIRMING LOVE

We love him, because he first loved us. 1 John 4:19

When we seek God's knowledge, we will find that God loves us. When did God start loving us? When did God start loving you? From the beginning before we ever existed.

We generally love those who loves us. God has loved us from the very beginning. You and I are special to him. Not only are you very special to God but everyone who is special to you is special to him. Your life is not by chance, and there is no accident of birth or life, that you are alive today. Right now, God is seeking you and God wants quality time with you, God always has, and God always will.

That verse is so definitive and absolute there should be evidence to prove it. And thank God there is. The Apostle Paul's introduction to the Athenians was a revelation of God. He had this to say to men and women seeking to worship, know and understand a God who was too mysterious and foreign to them. They recognized him as an "Unknown God." God, however, wants to be known and not hidden.

So Paul, standing before the council, addressed them as follows: "Men of Athens, I notice that you are very religious in every way, for as I was walking along I saw your many shrines. And one of your altars had this inscription on it:

'To an Unknown God.'

This God, whom you worship without knowing, is the one I'm telling you about. "He is the God who made the world and everything in it. Since he is Lord of heaven and earth, he doesn't live in man-made temples, and human hands can't serve his needs—for he has no needs. He himself gives life and breath to everything, and he satisfies every need. From one man he created all the nations throughout the whole earth. He decided beforehand when they should rise and fall, and he determined their boundaries. "His purpose was for the nations to seek after God and perhaps feel their way toward him and find him—though he is not far from any one of us. For in him we live and move and exist.

As some of your own poets have said, 'We are his offspring.' And since this is true, we shouldn't think of God as an idol designed by craftsmen from gold or silver or stone.

"God overlooked people's ignorance about these things in earlier times, but now he commands everyone everywhere to repent of their sins and turn to him. For he has set a day for judging the world with justice by the man he has appointed, and he proved to everyone who this is by raising him from the dead." *Act 17:22-31 NLT*

God is our father, even if you never knew your human father and God is wanting you to know him better. God is constantly revealing his love to you. This book is part of his great love letter to you.

You are intended to read it and receive his message of promise and hope and to be encouraged. This book is God's invitation for you to remember your creator, to honor his Sabbath which he established to connect us to him forever. It is an important reminder to "Save the Date." What date? The Sabbath Day.

Why is the Sabbath so special? Because God established it to prove that we belong to him and prove that he alone has a plan for our good. I assure you that God has a message for you and a blessing for you in the Sabbath that is life changing and will inspire you with hope for the future.

You may ask what is the Sabbath? Well let me help you understand by comparison. Believers in Christ thoroughly find absolute consensus when it comes to Prayer and its significance to the body of Christ. None would dare to openly belittle the importance of prayer or the power of it. They hold to it, cherish, preach, write about and even teach prayer.

I was seeking to explain the topic of Prayer to a group of Young People during a Zoom session that became common practice during the height of the COVID Pandemic. I took my inquiry to the internet. And found a definition of prayer that reflected a more universal yet not generic description of it. I will paraphrase below based on the inspiration that I found on the internet.

What is prayer? The most basic definition of prayer is "talking to God." Prayer is not meditation or passive reflection; it is direct address to God. It is the communication of the human soul with the Lord who created the soul. Prayer is the primary way for the believer in Jesus Christ to communicate his emotions and desires with God and to fellowship with God.

That sounds beautiful to me and while it alludes to the source of Prayer's power, it also begs the absolute question to me: why is it that we are divided upon the Sabbath. If I am asked what is the Sabbath? I would not find such and accepted or inspiration of it that I found for prayer.

Globally we liken the importance of Prayer, Worship and Church attendance as universally accepted and significant to Man. Although all do not pray to Jesus Christ, I will be speaking as a believer in the Son of God who also declared himself to be Lord of the Sabbath.

In review prayer worship and Church attendance are seen as drawing upon the power of the Most High our Creator who has all authority in Heaven and on Earth and the keys to life. Then the most basic definition of the Sabbath has been ignored and trivialized by all believers and this is a serious problem.

I was inspired to borrow from the prayer definition and by the Holy Spirit's inspiration express a definition of the Sabbath's significance and its beauty.

The most basic definition of the Sabbath is "Resting with God". Sabbath rest is not meditation or passive reflection or a nap time; it is a full surrender of the will by a man or woman to God. It is the exhale of the passions and desires of a human soul into the confidence of our Creator for renewal and refreshing.

It is waiting on the Lord who created the soul. It is the inhale of the Grace of God's promises and life affirming faith. It is closing our eyes to the world around us and opening them to the beauty of holiness, wholeness, freedom and release from our daily burdens. The Sabbath is Holy, it is the primary and preferred place of habitation for the believer in God as creator.

The Sabbath is where the sinful and the righteous are openly invited to come into a secure place and be reclaimed and restored in harmony with the will of the Creator of Life. The will of a triune God. The trinity known as God the father, God the Son Jesus Christ and God the Holy Ghost.

The Sabbath is a sacred provision that provides for our needs and promises that our prayers are heard and promises that our hopes are well founded and that we can have true fellowship with God.

The Sabbath is a reminder of all of this, and we must remember its significance. We should be encouraged by it. So, if that sounds good, we should not reject it and instead we can begin to discuss a distinction that is available for all to acknowledge.

The Sabbath is not faith, and it is not a practice or belief it is the arena where our faith can truly be satisfied.

My very thesis is based on what Christ claimed long after the creation of the world. What Christ said, to Sabbatarians regarding the Sabbath. He assured them that God desires mercy. He assured them that the Sabbath is a gift of God for Man's benefit a true manifestation of God's Love, Mercy and Grace and he insisted he was the very administrator of that Covenant of Love, Mercy and Grace.

"If you had known what these words mean, 'I desire mercy, not sacrifice,' you would not have condemned the innocent. For the Son of Man is Lord of the Sabbath." Matthew 12:7-8 NIV

"And he said unto them, The Sabbath was made for man, and not man for the Sabbath: Therefore the Son of man is Lord also of the Sabbath." Mark 2:27-28.

And he said unto them, "That the Son of man is Lord also of the sabbath." Luke 6:5

Simply put, Jesus Christ is our Sabbath, He is our Salvation an offering of peace. The Sabbath is in Christ and Christ spirit is in the Sabbath promising us Salvation and everlasting life. Reassuring us of the perfection of the Love of God which extends to every man, woman and child his great provision.

CHAPTER 3

ALL ABOUT JESUS

"Search the scriptures; for in them ye think ye have eternal life: and they are they which testify of me."
John 5:39

This book is a call to worship God our father as our creator. The message is that Jesus Christ is the answer! Jesus Christ is the Savior of the world. He is worthy of your consideration. He is worthy of your worship, devotion and praise. He is the key to your salvation and mine. He is also Lord of the Sabbath, so he is the reason for our worship

And a voice came out of the cloud, saying, "This is my Son, my Chosen One; listen to him!" Luke 9:35 ESV

A voice came from the cloud and said, "This is my Son. He is the one I have chosen. Obey him." Luke 9:35 ERV

I have been impacted by God's love in a very special way. I have not been his perfect child. I have not always been faithful and like the Prodigal Son I have learned that the God who loves you has been calling for me, persistently looking for me, and crying out to me to hear and remember that I am loved and important.

The truth is, my spiritual journey has been half hazard and transient? That is why I struggled? God has proven to me that my past paths were meaningless and did not lead me to freedom or enlightenment. My hope was only realized when I stopped, looked and listened for his voice and he was there to guide me back to him.

The message that he has given me to share is an invitation for you to know and experience his great love more intensely. His pleasure is to see us free and happy in his presence as we worship him with truly grateful hearts.

Whether you know this or not, Jesus did not put us in our messy state. Jesus saves us from ourselves and this world's chaos. Like me, whether you are religious or not, you are a sinner. Even if you are concerned or not, I am very certain that you know what is meant by that damning statement. We all understand what it is to be called a sinner.

To be called a sinner simply means that you and I are otherwise spiritually misaligned from God. So much so that we chose separation from God and are left to his judgment. I want you to know that even the sinner has hope, for we all are sinners. This same Jesus is everyone's savior. Now that is very good news for you and me.

"And from Jesus Christ. He is the faithful witness to these things, the first to rise from the dead, and

the ruler of all the kings of the world. All glory to him who loves us and has freed us from our sins by shedding his blood for us. He has made us a Kingdom of priests for God his Father. All glory and power to him forever and ever! Amen."
Revelations 1:5-6

Jesus Christ willingly came into the world on a mission of Love to save the dying and to remove the power and curse of sin. He alone can fix you. He wants to save and to heal you. The real question is how well do you know Jesus? Are you even willing to come to him for salvation? Would you choose Life or Death?

"Put all your rebellion behind you, and find yourselves a new heart and a new spirit. For why should you die, O people of Israel? I don't want you to die, says the Sovereign LORD. Turn back and live!" Ezekiel 18:31-32NLT

I am reminded that many times when I speak of traveling out of town and out of the state on business or for some unique event that those who I inform of my travel will often casually invite me and suggest that if or when I come to their area, I should contact them and or visit them. It is very interesting how far I have to come to get a chance to possibly see them.

Rare is the request or urgency expressed to come to see me even when I have come so far. Rare are the anxious inquiries that show a desire or preparation or anxious expectation for an opportunity to see me. I know it's not the same, but I am just saying.

"The true light was coming into the world. This is the true light that gives light to all people. The Word was already in the world. The world was made through him, but the world did not know him. He came to the world that was his own. And his own people did not accept him.

But some people did accept him. They believed in him, and he gave them the right to become children of God. They became God's children, but not in the way babies are usually born. It was not because of any human desire or plan. They were born from God himself. The Word became a man and lived among us. We saw his divine greatness— the greatness that belongs to the only Son of the Father. The Word was full of grace and truth." John 1:9-14 ERV

"But he was pierced for our rebellion, crushed for our sins. He was beaten so we could be whole. He was whipped so we could be healed. All of us, like sheep, have strayed away. We have left God's paths to follow our own. Yet the LORD laid on him the sins of us all." Isaiah 53:5-6 NLT

Our indifference has been our luxury. We have focused on ourselves and not Christ sacrifice so instinctively we lose sight of His importance. I am fully aware that many who will read this may claim to already know Jesus and have fellowship with Christ. Many will insist that they believe in God, and claim to worship God, but the truth is, the Devil and his Angles also believe.

"You believe that there is one God. That's fine! The demons also believe that, and they tremble with

fear. "James 2:19

Here is something I would like to share to set your minds in order and put things in the proper spiritual context when reading the remainder of this book.

1. Jesus Christ is everything to mankind – my Bible says that he is the Alpha and the Omega, The Almighty. *Ref Revelations 1:8; 21:6, 22:13*
2. Jesus is the only way – *Ref John 14:6*
3. God loves the World so much; he has given us his son Jesus Christ as a sacrifice for the sins of the entire World – *Ref John 3:16-18*
4. You must first believe that Jesus is God and accept that he is your savior to avoid eternal death – *Ref John 8:24; 11:25; John 20:31*
5. We are indebted to our Creator and owe our worship and praise to him for he created all things and came to restore us to our Heavenly Father as sons and daughters. *– Ref John 1:12-14; 17:3; Revelations 4:11*
6. We are offered pardon and forgiveness thru our faith and belief in Jesus Christ alone. We all require this forgiveness because we all have sinned. *– Ref Romans 3:22-28; I John 1:9*
7. There is but one God who is our creator and who can save you and remove the stain of your guilt and past sins and every knee will be bowed before him in the last day to acknowledge his righteousness in judgement

of the wicked who choose not to come to him in humility and Who choose not to be saved. *Ref Romans 14:10-12; Isaiah 45:20-24.*

Before you read any further, I invite you to take your Bible and look-up and read each referenced verse because that is the foundation of God's message, and it will help you prove the truth of anything that I will have written and that you will read. The word of God is your safeguard so let's see how God views that approach.

"The people of Berea were more open-minded than the people of Thessalonica. They were very willing to receive God's message, and every day they carefully examined the Scriptures to see if what Paul said was true." Acts 17:11 GW.

You and I can no longer afford to be aloof and stand-offish when it comes to the truth. We must seek the truth and we should be drawn to it and pursue it.

CHAPTER 4

IGNORANCE

"To the Law and to the testimony! If they do not speak according to this Word, it is because no light is in them." Isaiah 8:20 MKJV.

Ignorance is not bliss. There is a theme and certainly a verse in the Bible that declares that there is a way that seems right to a man, woman or child but that path leads to death *Ref Proverbs 16:25.*

No one is immune to ignorance: Not preachers, teachers, elders deacons, deaconesses, ushers, lawmakers, theologians, prophets, priest, kings, you or me. We all suffer from this plaque and yet we can all escape it when there is opportunity to know better and do better and we choose to do so.

This means there are choices we consciously make that are as deadly as drinking tainted water or breathing contaminated air. They may seem natural, reasonable, even necessary and safe but they ultimately yield the most tragic consequences: contamination, disease, pain, dying and ultimately death. What we don't know can kill us.

Today many are dying and destroying themselves without awareness or remedy. Their involuntary and subliminal impulses often influence their perception and dictate "needs" that are really just "wants".

Our choices are often made to pacify our lust and desires and are only exposed later by their poor consequences. Ultimately our greatest and most memorable disappointments are revealed when our ignorance has been removed by awareness and truth.

God has given us the ability to seek out any matter for understanding. It's no different than our reaction after tripping unexpectedly and looking back. We want to see what caused us to trip. Could we have avoided it? We are even more careful in the future.

Even a small skin prick is not ignored if it is unexpected. Pain and discomfort alert us. We try to identify the source. Shouldn't we find the source and understand our condition. Shouldn't we explore the experience and seek a remedy even if it seems unavoidable?

Yes, we collect and gather facts we consult, and we familiarize and then we come to conclusions so that we can understand our circumstances or comprehend causation and consequence.

Free choice is our highest privilege and honor. Man is the superior creation to all other animals both intellectually and spiritually. God created humankind in the image of God. *Ref Genesis 1:26-28.*

There is both a power and privilege that we all share, and that is free will and choice. This is the beginning of our self-determination. This was how God honored us. But with such power there is potential for error and a demand for accountability.

God put laws into existence to preserve us within our purpose. We are free to break or attempt to defy these laws at our own risk. On the other hand, we can thrive thru our awareness and willingness to work in harmony with those laws. We can do this in our best interest and honor our creator. I assure that God loves our ability to choose.

"So fear the LORD and serve him wholeheartedly. Put away forever the idols your ancestors worshiped when they lived beyond the Euphrates River and in Egypt. Serve the LORD alone. But if you refuse to serve the LORD, then choose today whom you will serve. Would you prefer the gods your ancestors served beyond the Euphrates? Or will it be the gods of the Amorites in whose land you now live? But as for me and my family, we will serve the LORD." Joshua 24:14-15 NLT

Knowing the hazards of ignorance, we must do all that we can to resist its numbing affects. Just because we feel good and comfortable not knowing does not mean there are no consequences to that temporary peace and ease that comes with it.

Driving with a leaking radiator on a long trip with hills

and distant gas stops will be a recipe for disaster. Being unaware makes it tragically disappointing when the consequence appears suddenly and with minimal warning far too late.

Some have sought enlightenment, with many pursuing it thru foreign and exotic religions even championing drug use as a catalyst and today we live in a so called "woke" culture boasting that we're not afraid to challenge the norms of the past by breaking the silence and uncovering past sins of our era.

There are necessary corrections but not all are correctable by verbal agreement only. Everyone living their truth but many without a clue of what the true truth really is or means. If you have been living your truth, I ask you how has that been working? Certainly, if God's truth is not the most important then it can't be working all the great.

Joshua cited the past history of fallen nations on both sides of the river Jordan and including the Red Sea. He knew the right God and that is the God he chose to serve. We all have a choice and ignorance should not be one of them.

CHAPTER 5

FOR OUR GOOD

But Joseph replied, "Don't be afraid of me. Am I God, that I can punish you? You intended to harm me, but God intended it all for good. He brought me to this position so I could save the lives of many people." Genesis 50:19-20 NLT

God has planned for our future. He is interested in our survival. God's great provision is the answer to our every need, known or unknown. I want to introduce you to Jesus Christ as Lord of all and Jesus Christ as the greatest provision to humankind and for humankind. God had a plan for us, and it is realized as we come to know Jesus.

God approved his own great plan for his creation when he called it "Very Good" **Ref Genesis 1:31** It is my contention that this expression proves that God already had a plan that was very good and that was why he could be satisfied with his creation. This is certified by what he did next.

"And God saw everything that he had made, and behold, it was very good. And the evening and the morning were the sixth day." Genesis 1:31

What God did next is critical to our future.

"Thus the heavens and the earth were finished, and all the host of them. And on the seventh day God ended his work which he had made; and he rested

on the seventh day from all his work which he had made. And God blessed the seventh day, and sanctified it: because that in it he had rested from all his work which God created and made." Genesis 2:1-3.

This completion of Creation and final act in establishing a day appended to Creation, highlights the Creator and his Creation. It demonstrates the wisdom and power of God and the persistence of God's love. Showing persistence in establishing a cycle that is only complete as it brings us to focus on our Creator.

This was the formal establishment of the weekly cycle. This was a proviso and a provision which I will try to demonstrate.

God's provisions in the created world would benefit man before and after sin but his provision of himself is essential for eternity. That provision was not a creation but reflection of the Creator's omniscient care and concern for his creation which he loved. It was all signified in a single day. It not only completed his creation but established a permanent link preserving and validating God's claim that we belong to him and justifying any future actions of God on our behalf.

In Six Days, God created but the Seventh Day God ceased to Create. The Sabbath is emblematic of Rest and a signature of God's completed Creation. If you are like me, you hardly can rest when things are unsettled or incomplete. We think about them in our sleep because we are fatigued but that is an element born out of sin. God ceased because nothing was unsettled. His creation was perfect and complete. God's rest demonstrated satisfaction with a plan that was executed to perfection.

If you would embrace the Sabbath, you would agree with the significance of the Sabbath for your good and you would desire to experience that kind of Grace that provides rest and peace. You would see the beauty of what the Sabbath is and who God is and, desire to worship the Lord of the Sabbath on the Sabbath.

To truly understand and experience the Sabbath has been a longing for me when the mere formality and structure and rigidness that I had learned had begun to wear away at me.

The Sabbath as an obstacle and hinderance could not inspire my obedience. Instead, it became an obstruction of the very God who purposed from the beginning to make a way of escape for me. Thru the Sabbath God shows his willingness to forgive and his desire to save.

"Therefore, you Israelites, I will judge each of you according to your own ways, declares the Sovereign LORD. Repent! Turn away from all your offenses; then sin will not be your downfall. Rid yourselves of all the offenses you have committed, and get a new

heart and a new spirit. Why will you die, people of Israel? For I take no pleasure in the death of anyone, declares the Sovereign LORD. Repent and live! Ezekiel 18:30-32 NIV

I had lost sight of the life and freedom that God promises for those who desire to choose God's way and to repent and obey. But I now see God's love when I now choose to obey and to worship the creator of all things. He is worthy of worship.

CHAPTER 6

THE DEEP FAKE

You have six days each week for your ordinary work, but the seventh day is a Sabbath day of complete rest, an official day for holy assembly. It is the LORD's Sabbath day, and it must be observed wherever you live. Leviticus 23:3 NLT

The Sabbath as a day of rest is not often disputed. 1 in 7 appears to be the fad interpretation. The significance of the day is certainly marginalized by current traditions because it avoids prioritizing God's intention to appease our convenience. It has become a social construct masquerading as truth. 1 in 7 is not the same as the 7th day Sabbath. It is a deep fake of major proportions.

Curiously as the world slides into chaos and desperation. We are seeing negative returns on our maximized labor and minimized rest. Family time and leisure have all but dissipated and worship is simply a timeslot within our day to get thru like a meeting that is unimportant. We are seeing burnout, broken relationships, clinical depression, emotional instability, increased violence, and suicides.

Church attendances have fallen consistently and those that do continue to be worshipers and who promote spirituality are often thought to be fanatics or out of touch with reality. Agnosticism has also impacted religion to the point that many who are religious turn on each other to point blame or to at least distance themselves from what are seen as fringe beliefs or proof of error, and it is not done in love.

We attack each other "We are better than them" or "beware of those people". We pride ourselves saying "They are wrong" while never asking am I wrong or how am I right? It's spiritual "Gas Lighting".

No one looks at what is happening today and ask what's wrong? Very few are turning to God and for those who claim faith in God, the standard of practice versus profession rings hollow because we no longer rely on God's standard to justify our actions. Instead, we manipulate scripture to affirm error rather than seek to know the truth. We take pride in numbers and assimilate with the masses like lemmings streaming off a cliff. We have forgotten God!

"My people are foolish and do not know me," says the LORD. "They are stupid children who have no understanding. They are clever enough at doing wrong, but they have no idea how to do right!"
Jeremiah 4:22

"My people bend their tongues like bows to shoot out lies. They refuse to stand up for the truth. They

only go from bad to worse. They do not know me,"
says the LORD. Jeremiah 9:3

If we do not know the truth, then we do not know God and if we do not know God then what do we really know?

It's hard to remember what you have never experienced. Hard to keep what was never yours. Hard to know what you have never been taught or to explore without curiosity or a desire to learn.

What do you know about the Sabbath which is God's special day?

So, you might be wondering what about the Sabbath can change and help us to begin to know God? Well, I am glad you asked.

God has been reconciling the world through Jesus Christ. God's love is revealed in the message of Christ and the claims that he himself made and the Sabbath was highlighted by Christ to show his mission, his authority and more.

"And haven't you read in the law of Moses that the priests on duty in the Temple may work on the Sabbath? I tell you, there is one here who is even greater than the Temple! But you would not have condemned my innocent disciples if you knew the meaning of this Scripture: 'I want you to show mercy, not offer sacrifices.' For the Son of Man is Lord, even over the Sabbath!" *Matthew 12:5-8 NLT*

This is the Gospel. This is the work of God, and this is

the passion of Christ to save and to deliver but more importantly, <u>this is not the work of man.</u>

This is not our work or our charge. We, like Christ disciples, stand condemned, but only Christ can declare our innocence. A condemned man or woman has no destiny that they look forward to but if they are declared innocent, all hope is realized.

We can seek relief from our suffering, and we can seek wisdom over ignorance and error. We can choose life instead of death.

The Lord of the Sabbath inspires hope and promises forgiveness to all who desire its. The Sabbath allows us to affirm our faith in the God who has provided such a wonderous reminder of his love. His love covers our error and our failures, not his. Shouldn't we desire to know him better? Shouldn't we seek him with all our heart and soul like David?

"O God, you are my God; I earnestly search for you. My soul thirsts for you; my whole body longs for you in this parched and weary land where there is no water. I have seen you in your sanctuary and gazed upon your power and glory.

Your unfailing love is better than life itself; how I praise you! I will praise you as long as I live, lifting up my hands to you in prayer. You satisfy me more than the richest feast.

I will praise you with songs of joy. I lie awake thinking of you, meditating on you through the night. Because you are my helper, I sing for joy in the shadow of your wings. I cling to you; your strong right hand holds me securely." *Psalms 63:1-8* NLT.

Jesus Christ is our Sabbath. He is our resting place. We all have labored in vain. We strive to master our fate and to shape our destiny, but we have no way to secure it. The burdens, the bruises and scars of our efforts and failures are not enough to cleanse us. We are not even required to forgive ourselves as many say we should.

A man, woman or child who harm themselves intentionally or not, cannot apologize to themselves for their self-harm or forgive themselves. They must seek correction and healing and begin to nourish themselves. We belong to God and as God's we confess and repent to God and any others we have harmed. God forgives us and removes our guilt.

Truly we were born sinners and we multiply our sins daily. God's love and Christ's blood alone, cleanses us. Our only hope is in the Lord of the Sabbath.

CHAPTER 7

THE INVITATION

"Then Jesus said, "Come to me, all of you who are weary and carry heavy burdens, and <u>I will give you rest</u>. Take my yoke upon you. Let me teach you, because I am humble and gentle at heart, and <u>you will find rest for your souls</u>. For my yoke is easy to bear, and the burden I give you is light." Matthew 11:28-30 NLT

If your sin burden is more than you can bear, seek the relief that only Jesus can offer and deliver. While studying this book you will come to see that Christ alone is your hope and glory. Like me, you will desire to reach that place of rest. You will want to taste and experience that goodness that is offered. You will seek to learn more about the rest and peace that God not only offered but promised from the very beginning when he gave us The Sabbath.

"Taste and see that the LORD is good. Oh, the joys of those who take refuge in him!" Psalms 34:8 NLT

"Calamity will surely destroy the wicked, and those who hate the righteous will be "punished. But the LORD will redeem those who serve him. No one who takes refuge in him will be condemned." Psalms 34:21-22 NLT

The Sabbath is a time and place of refuge. When the Sabbath is discussed, it is quite compelling and yet polarizing. It is often met with a quick dismissal and denial of its Biblical significance while embraced for its notable qualities and promise as a day of rest. It is all but ignored as a day that has a precise context in the plan of salvation and in the faith of Jesus Christ.

Yes, what is it about the Sabbath that separates us? The Sabbath's true purpose brings us together. We are all sinners and descendants of one man and woman and one God yet today there are so many who profess a belief and faithfulness to God in so many ways, expressions, and denominations.

There is no righteous history in the men and women who are seen as founding any of these religious movements only reference points. The critical message to uncover is the faith of the believers. Their faith must reach beyond their denominational ties and be linked to God who gave it.

"For by the grace given me I say to every one of you: Do not think of yourself more highly than you ought, but rather think of yourself with sober judgment, in accordance with the faith God has distributed to each of you." Roman 12:3 NIV

Each believer's response to God must stand the test of God's word apart from their affiliation. How are there any protestants without Martin Luther and several other pioneers who hazarded their lives to make the word of God accessible to the common man, woman, or child?

Today We hate to be denied anything, yet we do not treasure the word of God enough to study or begin to comprehend how powerful and liberating it is for those who have ignorantly followed traditions without comprehension only to finally learn the truth plainly in God's word.

Should we all be Lutherans, Tyndalens, Hussens, or should we all serve the God of those spiritual giants of that age? Is it not God who is speaking to us in the Bible? Praise God for the sacrifices of men and women of a by gone era to usher us into this current era of Bible proliferation as well as freedom of religion to worship God our creator with a clear conscience as we can in America and some other places in the world.

They accomplished this by their obedience to God and that was purpose enough for their thankless efforts. I am convinced that God's plan has always been to provide us with what we need to please him.

The Sabbath is about us coming to Christ. Coming together to meet our maker. Preparing us for greater than we have ever experienced without it. God has invited sinners to keep his Sabbath. How can we turn down such an invitation?

"For since the beginning of the world men have not heard, nor perceived by the ear, neither hath the eye seen, O God, beside thee, what he hath prepared for him that waiteth for him." Isaiah 64:4

But as Scripture says: "No eye has seen, no ear has heard, and no mind has imagined the things that God has prepared for those who love him." 1 Corinthians 2:9 GW

CHAPTER 7

REAL FAITH

"For I determined not to know anything among you, save Jesus Christ, and him crucified."
1 Corinthians 2:2

I believe the biggest error that any believer can make is to believe their mission and calling is to convince other believers that their church affiliation is wrong. I believe their calling is to encourage sincere study of the word of God. Faith comes by hearing and hearing by the word of God. *Ref Romans 10:17.*

It is the word of the Lord that agitates and imparts faith in Man. To know God is to know truth. Jesus Christ says *"...sanctify them through thy truth: thy word is truth." John 17:17.*

- To Sanctify = Set apart for a holy purpose. God's word is the beginning of all truth and everything that exist. *"By the word of the LORD were the heavens made; and all the host of them by the breath of his mouth"* Psalms 33:6.

The Sabbath commandment *Exodus 20:4-8* affirms this truth found in Genesis 2:3 *"And God blessed the seventh day and sanctified it: because he had rested from all his work which God created and made."*

- As believers, are we not to remain in agreement with the word of God and affirm that which is true? So, what is the problem with the "Sabbath" or "Sabbath keepers"? *"Finally, brethren, whatsoever things are true, whatsoever things*

37

are honest, whatsoever things are just, whatsoever things are pure, whatsoever things are lovely, whatsoever things are of good report; if there be any virtue, and if there be any praise, think on these things." Philippians 4:8

- What is not lovely about the Sabbath?

There will always be challenges of faith that every believer must be confronted with. Where is the hope and meekness and fear that Peter describes? **Ref 1 Peter 3:15**

"Examine yourselves, whether ye be in the faith; prove your own selves. Know ye not your own selves, how that Jesus Christ is in you, except ye be reprobates? But I trust that ye shall know that we are not reprobates. Now I pray to God that ye do no evil; not that we should appear approved, but that ye should do that which is honest, though we be as reprobates. For we can do nothing against the truth, but for the truth." 2 Corinthians 13:5-8

Every believer must maintain a good conscience for it is not a church or a denomination that we are called to defend or answer for and hold true to. It is one's good conversation in Christ.

I do not say this to validate, perpetuate or justify any who may in fact be in error but to communicate a need for each believer to examine themselves to confirm and for refreshing of their faith. We need inspiration to redirect our own action and course re-aligning us with the scriptures thru the leading of the Holy Spirit. **Ref John 16:13**

My obedience and my faithfulness to what God reveals to me in his word is all that I can answer for. The real question I ask myself is: What is God saying? Then what am I hearing or understanding? So, what is my response? If my hearing is not clear and my understanding is not clear, then I should ask for God's wisdom and study until I receive it.

"If you need wisdom, ask our generous God, and he will give it to you. He will not rebuke you for asking." James 1:5

Abraham preached no sermons of warning or instruction as Noah did, but he lived out his devotion in earnest to God. Both were faithful and powerful witnesses who were also imperfect, yet they were honored by God.

The Gospel of salvation will be made evident through our obedience. The history of the Bible stories proves that obedience with an earnest conscience towards God is better than Sacrifice which has no conscience. **Ref I Samuel 15:22** Earnestness does not cover sin, only the blood of Christ is able to do that.

James could not make this clearer. **Ref James 2:18** To condemn the works of a man or woman and say they have no faith is like saying there is no accountability. Despite the empowering Gospel of Grace, to ignore God's word, to hear and not to do what God says or communicate what God says to you, denies faith, denies God and cheapens Grace, and nullifies the Gospel Christ proclaimed.

If your spouse does not act faithfully in your marriage covenant, you would question their devotion and love and call them unfaithful. Keeping the Sabbath is a covenant action of those who recognize that God ask us to keep it in remembrance, to reverence him in doing so and to honor it as Holy.

There is no fault to be found in those actions. Those who remember it are equally accountable to keep it as well as the rest of God's commandments. This does not discount or ignore or belittle the Grace of God any more than a spouse publicly wearing a wedding band conceals their behavior in the marriage relationship. In truth it only magnifies that a marriage relationship exists and subjects the behavior of the wearer to the appropriate scrutiny and perhaps skepticism.

If you can find God's word annulling the Sabbath or Fidelity in marriage, promoting dishonor to parents, encouraging idolatry, covering truth or making any of the Ten commandments void then you have only found a way to justify yourself and sinful desires and like the Laodiceans, believe you need nothing.

The word of God says that we must repent of sin for all have sinned. *Ref Romans 3:23.* Why is the word to be a lamp unto our feet and a light upon our path? *Ref Psalms 119:105.* To expose and reveal. Why is the Law compared to a mirror? *Ref James 1:23.* To inform and make us aware of our condition and appearance.

Sabbath keepers are not in any way immune to sin in all the other commandments and if they understand this then they condemn themselves in keeping the Sabbath as they break other commandments.

"For the person who keeps all of the laws except one is as guilty as a person who has broken all of

God's laws." *James 2:10 NLT*

Trust the word of God. It is no better for those who do not keep the Sabbath out of ignorance or who believe that in keeping another day they have established a better covenant. Now if they also affirm the other nine commandments must be kept, they are in error in excluding the one.

So as Paul the Apostle, a well-documented Christian and Sabbatarian wrote, ***"Who art thou that judges another man's servant? To his own master he standeth or falleth. Yea he shall be holden up: for God is able to make him stand...But why dost though judge thy brother? Or why dost though set at nought thy brother? for we shall all stand before the judgement seat of Christ? ...So then every one of us shall give account of himself to God"*** *Romans 14:4 -12.*

So as Lord of the Sabbath Christ promises both forgiveness to those he proclaims are without guilt and he also promises judgement to those who reject him and deny his authority.

"But all who reject me and my message will be judged on the day of judgment by the truth I have spoken." *John 12:48 NLT*

Just why is the Sabbath so important to faith? Perhaps you had never really considered the Sabbath. Many Sabbatarians like myself perhaps have never truly considered it either despite it being practiced as their faith distinction. I want to share the Sabbath as much more than a mere distinction but as a basis for our faith.

CHAPTER 8

LET GOD BE TRUE

"For what if some did not believe? shall their unbelief make the faith of God without effect? God forbid: yea, let God be true, but every man a liar; as it is written, That thou mightest be justified in thy sayings, and mightest overcome when thou art judged." Romans 3:3-4

I was born and raised to believe that the 7th Day which is Saturday has always been the Sabbath. Historically this has been documented and proven to be true. This is not a study to produce historical evidence. This is a testimony of Jesus Christ.

It is not my intention to prove the Sabbath's existence is true no more than it is my intent to prove that there are 7 days in a week. My desire is to encourage you to reconsider the Sabbath of our Lord and savior because we need to know God better. And if we did, we must also consider it a day of great importance to God.

I do know that I have long been fascinated by the theology of the Sabbath as God's holy day and yet most of the world as I know are no longer even acquainted with its significance. Most of the world does not seem to reverence it as a special day. I have certainly failed to fully reverence it and so I can begin from there. Even for those who once worshiped on the Sabbath and have failed to continue to do so rarely deny it to be the Sabbath.

I was raised a Sabbatarian, and just growing up with this knowledge has always stuck with me. At the very least, I remained confused at how a day I knew was set aside for worship was ignored by society and another day was distinguished as a day of worship for which there is no biblical agreement. This is also a historical fact. There are plenty of writings that can affirm this; so again, I will not attempt to republish them.

Have you ever received a belated birthday card to acknowledge your birthday? I have. A belated birthday card acknowledges that it was forgotten, and that the sender wanted you to know that they cared and loved you and hoped that your day was great. I did enjoy receiving those cards as well, but I can't recall anyone who sent it insisting that my birthday changed and would now be acknowledged on another day. Sunday worship is belated worship. Belated means that it is not the true day of worship just like a belated birthday card.

Today and in the past some calendars are and were daringly designed and reformatted to change the weekly order to align Sunday as the 7th Day of the week, a substitute Sabbath I suppose. This was a visual rebranding with one intent to recondition or make the change appear to be valid. Yes, a "Deep Fake"

So, someone knew better. Certainly, the calendars did not do this on their own and God had not miraculously restructured them to show the true Sabbath in conflict to His well-preserved biblical account. So, this pretend resolution only begs the question that I would like you to answer: "What is it about the Sabbath…?" Why is it being trivialized.

In an age of turmoil and unrest an appropriate irony, there has been a distinct and persistent effort to obscure the true Sabbath and day of rest. Over time what was more commonly accepted as the Sabbath day, has become obscured and even imperceptible. It seems the same can be said for the worlds view of God.

Jesus is a household name almost universally recognized, symbolic of good but not always reverenced as God with and for us. If we understood and truly accepted Jesus Christ today, we might all be Christians. As Christians, we should love the Sabbath.

If we study the word of God more carefully, we might all desire to keep the Sabbath. I say might because the first human pair were given a choice and despite being made perfect, they chose rebellion instead.

I once was in a store that had not only African garments, but it has a lot of herbal treatments and homeopathic curatives. A man rushed in with a since of urgency quickly getting to the point of his reason for entering.

He asked, "Do you have anything that I can take that will flush my system so that I can pass a drug test?" The attendant was calm and asked him, "What drugs are you trying to remove from your system?"

The man answered "Cocaine". The attendant indicated that there was nothing that he had for that purpose. They could only treat some damaging health impacts of drug abuse. The man quickly left obviously very disappointed.

Today we are living in the consequence of our Adam and Eve's choice and the choices of others before us. We have added to their poor choices our agreement by the choices that we ourselves have made. As I witnessed and reflected on that man's experience and watched him leave the store, indeed it was time for this man to make better choices. It is also time for us to make better choices.

It is very clear that forgetfulness has a price. There is a consequence to forgetting what is important. How strange it is for the Creator of the world to be largely diminished and ignored? I see a distinct parallel between the decline of the Sabbath and the decline of true Christianity. I am also reminded of Christ's thoughtful conversation with the Samaritan woman at the well.

"So tell me, why is it that you Jews insist that Jerusalem is the only place of worship, while we Samaritans claim it is here at Mount Gerizim, where our ancestors worshiped?"

Jesus replied, "Believe me, dear woman, the time is coming when it will no longer matter whether you worship the Father on this mountain or in Jerusalem. You Samaritans know very little about the one you worship, while we Jews know all about him, for salvation comes through the Jews. But the time is coming—indeed it's here now—when true worshipers will worship the Father in spirit and in truth.

The Father is looking for those who will worship him that way. For God is Spirit, so those who worship him must worship in spirit and in truth."

*The woman said, "I know the Messiah is coming—
the one who is called Christ. When he comes, he
will explain everything to us." Then Jesus told her,
"I AM the Messiah!" John 4:20-26 NLT.*

Christ indicated that ignorance of God leads to
confusing and false worship. On the other hand, false
worship reinforces our ignorance of God. A false
Sabbath cannot promote the true Sabbath, nor can it
change the true Sabbath. So, the intention of the Deep
Fake is revealed.

God is looking for those who would desire to worship
as he desires to be worshiped and to recognize the
importance of true worship of God which is always to
the benefit of those who truly embrace the spirit of God
as they claim to embrace the Son of God.

Before the crucifixion of Christ, he had an audience
with Pilate to defend himself or to raise a defense
against the actions of his angry accusers who denied
him as God, but they went further to say that he was a
rebel and was trying to overthrow Rome and set himself
up as king.

Jesus said, *"My kingdom is not of this world. If it
were, my servants would fight to prevent my arrest
by the Jewish leaders. But now my kingdom is from
another place." "You are a king, then!" said Pilate.
Jesus answered, "You say that I am a king. In fact,
the reason I was born and came into the world is to
testify to the truth. Everyone on the side of truth
listens to me." Joh 18:36-37 NIV*

The problem is that we do not always listen to Christ,

we do not always seek the truth. Current events of these times have religious leaders from the Pope down engaged in dialogue acknowledging the need for a day of rest. This has been driven by our current world crisis (Including the Covid Pandemic) which has stimulated discussion of mental health and the need for societal awareness.

The Spiritual and moral decline of society and all governments around the world, combined with environmental erosion and systematic greed, have ushered in this new era and reality in pandemic proportions. Our ignorance, greed and false sense of security have run its course. Our unwillingness to learn the importance of spirituality and agreement with God has taken its toll on our lives and the lives of others including our environment.

Environmental pollution caused by machinery designed without those concerns and our continuous abuse of natural resources, have impacted our environmental health and are believed to be the root causes of global warming and climate change which are also associated with an escalation of catastrophic events in nature and around the world.

A Day of Rest is being encouraged around the world and 1 in 7 as previously stated seems to be popular and on the minds of many but with little thought of where this comes from. If it is to be considered, why is that day pointing to the first day of the week over the 7th day of the week? When I read and hear these things I am jolted into a reconsideration of the Sabbath and its importance in the word of God and to me.

CHAPTER 10

WHAT GOD SAYS

"Remember the Sabbath day by keeping it holy."
Exodus 20:8 NIV

If you have a guest who has a dietary restriction you do not ever try to ignore it and force them to eat what they do not or cannot eat. You certainly will not do that if you want them to continue to feel welcomed and loved. So, the Bible tells us what God wants and what God has to say about God, and we should listen and care.

We are particular about what behaviors we allow in our homes, cars, schools and courthouses and court rooms. We care about what matters to us. It's just a thought perhaps God matters to us. Perhaps Christ matters to us. The reason for his sacrifice was particular and he was found faithful because God mattered to him and we matter to God.

One day we will all be answering the question about what matters regarding important decisions that will have to be made. I cannot help but think about the Sabbath's importance to the world today. Perhaps, this is why God tells his people to remember the Sabbath Day. Perhaps it is because we are so forgetful, and God knows what our forgetfulness cost.

We humans are so particular about so much these days and diet is certainly one of those touchy subjects: Veganism vs Vegetarianism, Vegetarians that eat fish and eggs vs Meat eaters. Meat eaters that have a limited diet restricting to certain meats.

Wheat vs gluten free is yet another critical concern for some. Dairy vs the may substitutes. No one wants their dietary regimen compromised yet we seem to feel that God is not particular or purposeful. We often ignore what matter to God.

Exactly how does that work when we generally choose diet for health or to promote life. God gives us life and offers us eternal life, yet our worship apparently does not matter? Should God compromise and accept our alternatives? God desires that we change our priorities to align with his purpose for our lives.

Jesus prayed to his father for his disciples and followers, *"Sanctify them through thy truth: thy word is truth." John 17:17*

There is no shortcut to pleasing God. We must trust and obey. God even created the world by thru his Son which he has identified as the Word. We read earlier God ask us to listen to him.

"In the beginning was the Word, and the Word was with God, and the Word was God. The same was in the beginning with God. All things were made by him; and without him was not anything made that was made." John 1:1-3

I was taught to consider the Bible as the word of God. It is God's message to all of mankind. God used men to write and communicate his message in ways that we can relate. God's messengers are called Prophets and, in some cases, literal angels were also used to share his important messages to men and women. What is just as significant is the fact that God's word tells us that Jesus Christ is the Word of God. Jesus Christ is the Word, and the Word is truth.

Anyone who believes this to be true is more than capable of learning about what God reveals in his word. God's intent to communicate to Man is for the good of mankind. The essence of the Word of God is to communicate God's love and affinity towards all of mankind.

The word of God reveals the heart and character of God and his matchless love. God is Good and his desire for the world is good. The Bible tells us of Jesus Christ, whose very own account, reveals God's love for us. From the beginning Jesus Christ was the Word of God and more.

So many in the world today have questioned God's love. Why? Because the earth is full of misery and darkness. Much of the suffering that exist requires a supernatural intervention to spare those who suffer or have been victimized.

While we have often ignored what God tells us is the right thing to do, we claim some authority over what the right thing is that God should do. If our way is really better, then why can't we fix our own problems and end our own suffering?

Many including Christians today reason that an All-Powerful God should prevent the spreading devastation. Why don't they consider the actions of an All-Loving God? We often do not do all that is within our power to prevent pain, suffering and hunger and we often fail to intervene on behalf of those we love who have chosen or acted unwisely on more than one occasion or have knowingly resisted our good counsel and well-intentioned efforts. Yet we dare to challenge God?

"Do you think that I like to see wicked people die? says the Sovereign LORD. Of course not! I want them to turn from their wicked ways and live. However, if righteous people turn from their righteous behavior and start doing sinful things and act like other sinners, should they be allowed to live? No, of course not! All their righteous acts will be forgotten, and they will die for their sins. "Yet you say, 'The Lord isn't doing what's right!' Listen to me, O people of Israel. Am I the one not doing what's right, or is it you?" Ezekiel 18:23-25 NLT.

Many in the world do not recognize that God suffers with us just as we suffer with others. It is God's pain to see us suffer and because of his love God does not always intervene and prevent our pain and suffering but none the less, God is with us and suffers thru our pain. Why? Because God will not remove our choice.

"God loved the world this way: He gave his only Son so that everyone who believes in him will not die but will have eternal life. God sent his Son into the world, not to condemn the world, but to save the world. Those who believe in him won't be condemned. But those who don't believe are already condemned because they don't believe in God's only Son.

This is why people are condemned: The light came into the world. Yet, people loved the dark rather than the light because their actions were evil. People who do what is wrong hate the light and don't come to the light. They don't want their actions to be exposed." John 3:16-20 GW

I am thrilled that many have been persuaded thru diligent study of the Word of God and thru the charitable acts of Christian believers to turn their hope and trust to him. Many despite their circumstance cling to their budding faith in Jesus Christ hoping for the promise of his return and his reward for those who trust in him although they suffered and or died because of their faith. God will not be pleased by our lack of faith but when presented with evidence of his great love for us, God will bring us into conformity with his will and save many who would otherwise be lost.

"Brothers and sisters, we do not want you to be uninformed about those who sleep in death, so that you do not grieve like the rest of mankind, who have no hope."

"For we believe that Jesus died and rose again, and so we believe that God will bring with Jesus those who have fallen asleep in him. According to the Lord's word, we tell you that we who are still alive, who are left until the coming of the Lord, will certainly not precede those who have fallen asleep."

"For the Lord himself will come down from heaven, with a loud command, with the voice of the archangel and with the trumpet call of God, and the dead in Christ will rise first. After that, we who are

still alive and are left will be caught up together with them in the clouds to meet the Lord in the air. And so we will be with the Lord forever. Therefore encourage one another with these words." 1 Thessalonians 4:13-18 NIV.

There are some great revelations in the Bible. Jesus Christ is the great theme and thrust of the entire Bible. Christ's purpose was to reveal the love of the Father. Christ's mission was to do God's will as his son and redeem fallen man. This book will not reveal anything to the contrary but to highlight God's great provision for man. This great provision has withstood millenniums of sin and remains as a promise that God is truly with us and for us from the very beginning.

The name Emanuel, means God with us, was not just evidenced at Christ's birth or a set for a future date but from the beginning. It is the revelation of Jesus Christ as our creator and as our Sabbath before sin and the promise of a Messiah. It was the assurance of a great work long finished and a promise for a marred creation's renewal. This is why Christ declared himself "Lord of the Sabbath"

CHAPTER 11

THE PROVISION

"... The Sabbath was made for man, and not man for the Sabbath: Therefore, the Son of man is Lord also of the Sabbath." Mark 2:27-28

What about the Sabbath? Christ is in the Sabbath revealing that he is our Sabbath. What is it about the Sabbath that God must remind us to recall, remember and yes even reconsider? What would motivate anyone to ignore or distract us from the Sabbath? Well let's find out for ourselves.

There is something Special about the Sabbath that goes beyond the observance of the Day. The Sabbath was sanctified and set apart from the 6 literal days of creation by the creator. The Sabbath allows man to observe the Perfection and Holiness of the Creator's will and actions. The Sabbath is unique and special. For the Christian who is discerning, so it is important to take notice of wthat Jesus Christ said.

I read Christ's words regarding the Sabbath as meaning that Christ is synonymous with the Sabbath. Christ describes the Sabbath, not as a creative act of God but as an expression of the good will of God for all mankind. So, in saying that the Sabbath was "made" for mankind he is not describing it as a creation which was placed under man's dominion but was "made" a provision for man who was to be a steward of God's creation which was very good prior to man's fall.

The Sabbath is a reminder that God thru Christ sanctifies us and make us peculiar. The Sabbath proves that we are special to him. There is life assured in the relationship with God. The Sabbath is God's covenant with his Creation and Christ is the guarantor of this covenant. We know that with God all things have purpose and that he provides for our necessities and for our good. The Sabbath is God's perfect provision for mankind.

Let's look at the definition for that word "provision."

pro·vi·sion *

/prə'viZHən/

noun

1. *the action of providing or supplying something for use: "new contracts for the provision of services"*

Similar words: supplying; supply; providing; purveying

2. *an amount or thing supplied or provided: "low levels of social provision"*

Similar words: facilities; services; amenities; resources

verb

1. *supply with food, drink, or equipment, especially for a journey: "civilian contractors were responsible for provisioning these armies"*

2. **set aside an amount in an organization's accounts for a known liability: "financial institutions have to provision against loan losses"**

*Definition on the web powered by Oxford Dictionaries

Only the creator of all things can account for his creation making provision for its survival. Man was to be steward over the earth and yet because of free will and choice, man was more than capable of introducing sin into the world. But for the Grace of God, a provision was made for man to be restored and accepted by God.

"Remember to observe the Sabbath day by keeping it holy. You have six days each week for your ordinary work, but the seventh day is a Sabbath day of rest dedicated to the LORD your God. On that day no one in your household may do any work. This includes you, your sons and daughters, your male and female servants, your livestock, and any foreigners living among you. For in six days the LORD made the heavens, the earth, the sea, and everything in them; but on the seventh day he rested. That is why the LORD blessed the Sabbath day and set it apart as holy. Exodus 20:8-11 NLT.*

Such a reminder is essential for all of mankind and not just for the Jew. The Sabbath was intended for man and not man for the Sabbath. Christ is the reason for the Sabbath's importance. The Bible declares:

"In the beginning the Word already existed. The Word was with God, and the Word was God. He existed in the beginning with God. God created everything through him, and nothing was created except through him." John 1:1-3 NLT

"Thus the heavens and the earth were finished, and all the host of them. And on the seventh day God

*ended his work which he had made; and he rested
on the seventh day from all his work which he had
made. And God blessed the seventh day, and
sanctified it: because that in it he had rested from
all his work which God created and made."* Genesis
2:1-3 KJV

*"He also says to the Son, "In the beginning, Lord,
you laid the foundation of the earth and made the
heavens with your hands."* Heb 1:10 NLT

There is certainly evidence that Christ's role in Creation
supports his authority and reverence as God. It is also
clear that God the Father's will was expressed before
the creation of the world and that Christ fully fulfilled
that role as creator and savior in favor with God and for
the favor of man.

*"In the past God spoke to our ancestors at many
different times and in many different ways through
the prophets. In these last days he has spoken to us
through his Son. God made his Son responsible for
everything.*

*His Son is the one through whom God made the
universe. His Son is the reflection of God's glory
and the exact likeness of God's being. He holds
everything together through his powerful words.
After he had cleansed people from their sins, he
received the highest position, the one next to the
Father in heaven."* Heb 1:1-3 GW

Christ was made a provision for man's continued
existence. Not for any error of God but for the
potential error of man. The Bible assured us that death

was the penalty or result and the ultimate consequence of man's disobedience.

I have observed rock climbers at various stages of their climb and with exception of those that free climb without any protection, there is always evidence of preparation for their next step. There are often tethers and anchors to limit the impact of a misstep or free fall. This is clearly reflective of their awareness of the potential dangers.

With death as the consequence, what provision could sinful man make to cover his own sin from a God who sees all and knows all. Man did not know sin until he chose to disobey, there was no provision that man could make to avoid or safeguard against the unknown. Praise God! Only our creator could.

Man was introduced to the ceremony of offering a sacrifice of an innocent lamb as a substitutionary death symbolizing atonement for man's sin and not the animals.

God will not allow a subordinate sacrifice to atone for the ordinant, which is the death of the deserving. With man's dominion only over the created life he had nothing better to offer and could not be cleared of his own deserving death sentence. Nor could his death vindicate anyone else.

Christ was God's promised provision to man and therefore after the 6th day God rested. It was already determined and decided. God would provide for us. Abraham accurately surmized that any adequate sacrifice as an offering to God must be provided by God.

"Isaac spoke up and said, "Father?" "Yes, Son?" Abraham answered. Isaac asked, "We have the burning coals and the wood, but where is the lamb for the burnt offering?" Abraham answered, "God will provide a lamb for the burnt offering, Son." The two of them went on together." Genesis 22:7-8 GW

We are called to worship God, our creator. We are called to reverence him. We are called into his Holy presence to account for our choices. We must be prepared to give an answer. Abraham was found faithful to the God who provides. And God did provide.

"Do not lay a hand on the boy," he said. "Do not do anything to him. Now I know that you fear God, because you did not refuse to give me your son, your only son." When Abraham looked around, he saw a ram behind him caught by its horns in a bush. So Abraham took the ram and sacrificed it as a burnt offering in place of his son. Abraham named that place The LORD Will Provide. It is still said today, "On the mountain of the LORD it will be provided." Genesis 22:12-14 GW

The question now remains, why wouldn't we worship our creator? How should we worship our Creator? Was it left to us to figure out for ourselves? In asking us to remember, has God already ordained the appropriate time and place for worship? All of this is something you should consider beyond reading this book.

CHAPTER 12

WE DON'T KNOW

"Wherefore the Lord said, Forasmuch as this people draw near me with their mouth, and with their lips do honour me, but have removed their heart far from me, and their fear toward me is taught by the precept of men: Therefore, behold, I will proceed to do a marvellous work among this people, even a marvellous work and a wonder: for the wisdom of their wise men shall perish, and the understanding of their prudent men shall be hid. Surely your turning of things upside down shall be esteemed as the potter's clay: for shall the work say of him that made it, He made me not? or shall the thing framed say of him that framed it, He had no understanding?" Isaiah 29:13-14, 15

Can we agree that we are not God? Can we marvel at natures beauty and complexity? How was the human eye formed? As we begin to comprehend just how marvelous God's power and how he created all things, we can begin to recognize that God is like the Potter and certainly has more knowledge than his creation. Our purpose can only be unveiled by our maker.

Before sin, the Sabbath brought all of God's creation to rest before him. The Sabbath established a perpetual reminder that the Creator had provided all that we could ever need. It was a day to acknowledge and appreciate the Creator. Man's freedom was fully realized in the Sabbath even prior to sin. For on the 6th day God had completed his creation, for the Bible says God had finished. God declared his acts of creation good. God also considered what was good for man before completing his creation.

Then the LORD God said, "It is not good for the man to be alone. I will make a helper who is just right for him." Genesis 2:18

God after forming man by His will, fashioning Man in His image, God commissioned man to steward his creation, honoring man with dominion over every living animal on earth. God provided the ultimate provision for man, identifying his social nature and presented man with a woman to share in the process of procreation to complete the reproductive process. God introduced sexuality to satisfy and provide pleasure building a bond for the couple who were to multiply with offspring to fill this earth. God also provided for man's nourishment and sustenance, by establishing a diet to satisfy his appetite and a variety of flavors to taste and enjoy.

"Taste and see that the LORD is good. Oh, the joys of those who take refuge in him! Fear the LORD, you his godly people, for those who fear him will have all they need. Even strong young lions sometimes go hungry, but those who trust in the LORD will lack no good thing." Psalms 34:8-10

"The LORD God placed the man in the Garden of Eden to tend and watch over it." Genesis 2:15 NLT

Man was given an active and utilitarian purpose in advance of the Sabbath. Man would be pleased and experience the perfection of God's creative work. In the creation of the Woman for Man, here the intent of his Creator is shown to be good. God introduced the Sabbath, a Day that God provided for man: A special place and time for Man to take in the wonders of God and to bless the Lord, praise and worship his creator and God.

God, who spoke the world into existence and formed Man out of the dust and breathed into him "the breath of Life" ended his work of creation and with infinite wisdom established a day that is filled with expectation of hope and that is set aside for Man, the chief of God's creation. The creator has made it Holy uncorrupted and incorruptible for Man to experience and know both the Love and Power of God.

Surely, we have corrupted the earth by sin. Surely, we have tasted death and cannot further our life upon this earth instead we eventually turn to dust. Each day we live on this Earth we toil and labor for what we think we need, and we labor for what we desire. Our labors are in vain if we labor for our salvation. God ceased His labor but not without providing man an opportunity to cease from his labors as well.

The Sabbath is as irrefutable as the 7-day week. The week does not exist apart from the Sabbath. The Sabbath is the only day unimpacted by sin and the first question we must ask is, how is that? Why is it sanctified? How is it still Holy and what is the purpose of a Holy Day in a sinful world? What is its importance to sinful man? Well, it is God's great provision. By now we should know that Jesus Christ is God's provision.

"For God so loved the world, that he gave his only begotten Son, that whosoever believeth in him should not perish, but have everlasting life. For God sent not his Son into the world to condemn the world; but that the world through him might be saved. He that believeth on him is not condemned: but he that believeth not is condemned already, because he hath not believed in the name of the only begotten Son of God." Joh 3:16-18

Jesus Christ is the Sabbath for mankind and the Sabbath is rest. That rest dwells within Christ, therefore it is Holy. For Man, the Sabbath is a window into Christ's completed work. It is a refuge from our troubled lives. A door that leads into the realm of God's perfection. It is the promise that we are God's children and will be made whole by his will and power alone. Why the Sabbath? It is because God loves us.

As a parent I wanted to provide for my children. Before they were even born, I made preparations. All the lovely stuff that said I was excited and would love them, but I also had something that was essential for all of my children that proved that I would care for them, diapers.

Yes, it is not the pleasant brag like a trending top of the line stroller, crib or car seat which are more for vanity. Jesus Christ was born with none of those things he slept in an animal feed trough. I needed to be prepared to keep them not only safe, warm and fed but to clean them up and keep them fresh and dry.

Even our best provisions cannot compare to salvation. We have no righteousness and in case we believe that we do. The scriptures compare our so-called righteous ness to a filthy rag or even a badly soiled diaper if I may take a little liberty given my previous example.

We are all infected and impure with sin. When we display our righteous deeds, they are nothing but filthy rags. Like autumn leaves, we wither and fall, and our sins sweep us away like the wind. Isaiah 64:6 NLT

A time is coming that has been prophesied when God shall again gather his creation fully restored in a peaceful and perfectly joyful state united to worship the Lord of the Sabbath and of all creation for his goodness towards us. I believe no other day or time will be more joyous.

CHAPTER 13

THE DIFFERENCE

"You have six days each week for your ordinary work, but the seventh day is a Sabbath day of complete rest, an official day for holy assembly. It is the LORD's Sabbath day, and it must be observed wherever you live. Leviticus 23:3 NLT

Having concluded creation, it stands out that God should append a day for man's timeline that is outside of the previous 6 and outside of man's dominion. While in 6 days Everything that was made was made and pronounced completed by God. The 7th day was appended to the Creation week.

If Man was made Landlord of the earth, then the Creator of all things, is Lord alone of the Sabbath. The Sabbath is a day forever set apart yet forever united to the weekly cycle and clearly the first order of attention to man after discovering all that was created for him to be steward over. Man was steward of all things on earth but not the Sabbath. The Sabbath belongs to God and man was allowed to share in it for his benefit.

A fundamental truth that I have begun to understand is that God is even bigger and greater than I can suppose or imagine. I know for a fact that God is bigger and greater than you have comprehended. There is a certainty that I must express to you so that you will know it to be true as you read this. Before anything, the creation of our world and all that we can know within human existence to have been created, God simply is...

"My thoughts are nothing like your thoughts," says the LORD. "And my ways are far beyond anything you could imagine. For just as the heavens are higher than the earth, so my ways are higher than your ways and my thoughts higher than your thoughts." Isaiah 55:8-9 NLT

I say this because, per scripture it also appears that the Sabbath perfectly illustrates the eternal gospel and message Jesus Christ shared of the incomparable love of God towards the world. The Sabbath was not created when our world was formed. The Sabbath is Holy – Man cannot define or limit Holiness. Holiness is a God thing. The Sabbath is Sanctified or set apart for a Holy purpose. As Holy, the Sabbath is distinguished from any other day.

The Bible is distinct in describing the day in contrast with all the other days. The 24-hr. daily cycle which is characterized evening to morning, this period was established at the conclusion of the first day of creation and it is repeated Day 2 thru Day 6 only. The Seventh day is introduced but it is not quarantined in the same way as all the other days at its conclusion. The phrasing is clearly absent because nothing was created.

The significance of the Sabbath cannot be contained or limited to its relationship to the prior 6 days only. However, the period of its identification would be considered by man within the same time frame that God had set for man in separating each day. The significance of the 7th day is in how it relates to the Creator, God alone. The perpetuity of the Sabbath is a promise and source of hope for our salvation and renewal.

"Don't keep looking at my sins. Remove the stain of my guilt. Create in me a clean heart, O God. Renew a loyal spirit within me. Do not banish me from your presence, and don't take your Holy Spirit from me. Restore to me the joy of your salvation, and make me willing to obey you. Then I will teach your ways to rebels, and they will return to you." Psalms 51:9-13.

The Sabbath commemorates the inaction of God in relationship to God's explicit actions in the beginning of Creation and thru the Creation week. A week should be considered 6 Days, but the 7th Day is God's Holy Day. God established the week to be 7 days and not 6. In in this way the Sabbath was made for Man to remember his creator.

The Sabbath returns man's focus towards his Creator and is a welcome invitation for all who desire to remember him just as rest is a welcome experience for those who have lived and labored long. Like fruit on a vine, it gets sweeter with time. ***Ref Ecclesiastes 12:1***

The Sabbath remains in Christ and with Christ for he is our provider. The Sabbath brings Christ to our remembrance. Again, I say, the Sabbath was not created, nor did it signal the end of God's Creative power. In fact, it does not limit or stifle God's creative power but instead invites man to find his completion in his Creator and to experience the true power of God. It reconnects us to God's original plan.

The Sabbath is a provision of the Creator. The Sabbath's singularity is as unchangeable and undiminishable as it is unequivocal. It is God's great reveal to the world and a study of it and an application to it will reveal the Love of God, for man. God could not contain his love and enthusiasm for his creation so after the 6th day God promised us more than the world. The Sabbath is our reminder and assurance of God's love.

Who can pray or worship without a knowledge of God? Who can truly believe in salvation from sin without seeing an olive branch in the Sabbath day which is a sign of the peaceful intention of God towards us? It is a weekly relief and respite from our daily drudgery and the burden of work but more than that it is a promise of forgiveness of our sins.

God has provided this rest and relief. God will provide for our salvation. The Sabbath says God wants to continue to be our God despite our sins and poor choices. Oh, what a difference the Sabbath makes.

"This is the day which the LORD hath made; we will rejoice and be glad in it." Psalms 118:24

The Sabbath is not just any other day. If we love Christ, we will honor him as God. We will live in communion with God and live for God. We are reminded that we cannot take it for granted as any other day just as the day of our reunion when Jesus Christ returns will not be just any other day.

The day of deliverance is not just any other day. A day of rest after 6 days of labor is not just any other day. We anxiously await it, and we gratefully celebrate it.

We cry out that the Lord he is God! We cry out Holy, Holy, Holy! So even our thoughts and actions reflect reverence and Honor in His presence. We account ourselves as in the presence of God living and communicating reverently before him.

"Know ye that the LORD he is God: it is he that hath made us, and not we ourselves; we are his people, and the sheep of his pasture." Psalms 100:3

If the Priest daily efforts in the first compartment of the sanctuary were considered Holy, they pertained to the second compartment for which they entered only once a year which was the Holy of Holy. The High priest only could enter in and present before God an atonement offering of Blood Sacrifice for the people of God.

The temple must be cleansed of the guilt of the people. The Priest must present the required sacrifice, but God must accept it. Then the sin was to be transferred to the goat and God's people spared. Finally, that anxiety turned to relief and joy.

We are now in anxiety but all who live for God and love his Sabbath will live with respect to this time in anticipation of that great and final day when the High Priest of our Souls returns in the Clouds of Glory pronouncing God's favor to his faithful ones *"Well Done..." Ref Matt 25:21,23 and Heb 9:28.*

The is a distinction between days. Compared to the first six days of the week which are considered common as the began and ended in the same way, the Sabbath has nothing in common with them.

A school prom, a wedding and even a debutant ball have distinction and time is a critical factor. Their time and dates are set and confirmed. The tickets and guest list are distributed and all necessary preparations are made. Anyone attending will have chosen outfits and attire and been fitted well in advance. But despite all of that you absolutely cannot forget the day.

So no, this is not a small thing. It is not inconsequential, nor should it be trivialized as many attempt to do.

CHAPTER 14

SAFE HOUSE

"But now you are free from the power of sin and have become slaves of God. Now you do those things that lead to holiness and result in eternal life. For the wages of sin is death, but the free gift of God is eternal life through Christ Jesus our Lord." Rom 6:22-23 NLT

God would not have provided and introduced the Sabbath if we were only expected to continually live in sin, since sin is death to us. Sin expels us from the presence of our Holy Creator. Sin exiles us and reminds us we should be forever separated from our maker.

God provided the Sabbath so that we would be assured that He who created us can make us sinless and give us eternal life and a new beginning. God is love and the Sabbath is an eternal reminder of his love. The Sabbath invites us into God's will and that is for us to be in the presence of God.

"And I saw another angel fly in the midst of heaven, having the everlasting gospel to preach unto them that dwell on the earth, and to every nation, and kindred, and tongue, and people, Saying with a loud voice, Fear God, and give glory to him; for the hour of his judgment is come: and worship him that made heaven, and earth, and the sea, and the fountains of waters." Revelations 14:6-7

Jesus Christ is the gift God provided for mankind. Christ says that the Sabbath was made for Man and concluded that he was Lord of the Sabbath. Could it be clearer that God wanted to remind us of this fact as he called us to remember His Holy Day? Although we are sinful and we are unworthy, we are safe and can find welcome sanctuary in the Sabbath.

"The LORD says, "I will make a new world—new heavens and a new earth—that will last forever. In the same way, your names and your children will always be with me. Everyone will come to worship me on every worship day; they will come every Sabbath and every first day of the month." This is what I, the LORD, have said." Isa 66:22-23 ERV

Saturday is the 7th day completing the weekly cycle and is always preceded by Friday and followed by Sunday. This is how we know that Sunday is the 1st day of the week and not the 7th. The Bible says God told them to remember the Sabbath day. *Ref Exodus 20:8.* This reaffirms the preexistence of The Sabbath prior to the presentation of Ten Commandments. So, Genesis is where we must start.

The Sabbath preexist Judaism and all cultural distinctions. Jesus said that the Sabbath was made for Man, this only reaffirms his declaration as God. Christ was expressing a knowledge of God's will toward man, Christ confirmed that man was not made for the Sabbath. Jesus Christ also declared his authority over the Sabbath. Again, I associate Christ Authority as his authorship over all creation.

A man or woman is not made for the clothing, but clothing is made for them. If it doesn't fit, it is either useless or disregarded but when it is tailor made and custom fit it is worn with pride and not abused. When the man and woman found themselves naked, they hid and tried to make clothing for themselves out of fig leaves.

"Then the eyes of both of them were opened, and they realized they were naked; so they sewed fig leaves together and made coverings for themselves." Genesis 3:7 NIV

And the LORD God made clothing from animal skins for Adam and his wife." Genesis 3:21 NLT

Translation, when it is made for us it can suit us but by the change in tailor, God demonstrated that what he made for them, will benefit the most. What God provides is better than what we can or will attempt to do for ourselves. Adam and Eves effort was a show and tale while God made clothing with practical usefulness. That simple act is the action of a loving parent understanding that we would never be able to cover our mess properly.

"Made for Man", that is not only flattering to man, but it should also bring glory to God. Man is not defined as a Christian, Jew, Hebrew, or any other religious adherent.

Those who find the Sabbath a drudgery or a responsibility that hinders their freedom and burdens their lifestyle or flat out disrupts their traditions etcetera, have not observed it properly or comprehended what the Lord of the Sabbath intended. The Sabbath is our Safe House. It is to be our place of safety.

Every hard-working laborer understands the importance of a break. Breaks required in a day and breaks taken at the end of the week add benefit to our lives. They give place for reflection and thoughtful consideration of achievement. After sin, the Sabbath brings relief to all of God's creation, a respite, a day of rest and reflection. It is a day to appreciate that the Creator of all things has made provision for us to escape.

"The temptations in your life are no different from what others experience. And God is faithful. He will not allow the temptation to be more than you can stand. When you are tempted, he will show you a way out so that you can endure."
1 Corinthians 10:13 NLT

God has provided but sometimes we must be reminded, taught and instructed.

An Airplane steward or stewardess calls your attention to the safety provisions preinstalled or packaged in the airplane before they take to flight. They point to exits and the lighted aisle with key instructions in the event of an emergency. God calls us to remember the Sabbath day. He is showing us in the Sabbath how he has prepared in the event of a man-made emergency, courtesy of our poor choices.

I am convinced that to understand the significance of the Sabbath we must read the Bible to study it. The Creation story, the fall of man and the plan of redemption. We must identify the types and understand the epidemiology of sin. In doing this we will ultimately understand the importance of the Sabbath in the plan of Salvation.

The Sabbath is so much more than we comprehend. Those who come to truly seek it out will come face to face with our Creator. It is time that we begin to see how we have come to the place where we have forgotten God. It is amazing that the "created" has forgotten that we are created and forgotten our purpose because we have also forgotten the Sabbath.

Even Sabbatarians have confused their acceptance and acknowledgement of the Sabbath and God, as being the same as fulfilling our Creators ambition for them. So, in keeping the Sabbath, they are only addressing the part of it. Christ began his ministry with this declaration in the front of his church.

When he came to the village of Nazareth, his boyhood home, he went as usual to the synagogue on the Sabbath and stood up to read the Scriptures. "The Spirit of the LORD is upon me, for he has anointed me to bring Good News to the poor. He has sent me to proclaim that captives will be released, that the blind will see, that the oppressed will be set free, and that the time of the LORD's favor has come." Luke 4:16,18-19 NLT

The Sabbath speaks to God's love for the world and continually invites all to come and experience God's Love. If that is their priority, then God is glorified. If they only seek adherence to rules and regulations, they are in error. The Sabbath should serve the ministry of Christ example.

Those who keep it should be meek, humble and loving. We should be self-sacrificing and modeling the character of Christ instead of trying to prove how exacting we can be given our spiritual track record. We owe nothing to ourselves but to Christ.

We are either too busy or too defiant to stop, pause and wait on God to complete us. We are restless and dismissive, blind leading the blind because we have eyes but cannot not see. Ears but cannot hear. Lord have mercy. If only we would open our heart to God. If only we would allow ourselves to wonder, and he would reveal to us something so grand and special that we would be transformed.

CHAPTER 15

VERY GOOD

"And God saw everything that he had made, and, behold, it was very good..." Genesis 1:31.

Yes, God intended that man should honor him as Creator of all things seen and unseen which follows that with each day God brought honor to himself and on the 6th day God created a being in his image upon whom God honored with greater distinction.

God gave us dominion over our environment and allowed the first man to identify each creature culminating in the creation of the woman to partner with and to complete man. Man reveled in God's last creation thru whom God's love for man was clearly revealed.

Yes, the creation of woman revealed that God had concern for the good of man and that was only a glimpse of God's grand plan. God dropped the microphone and pronounced the following benediction. "Very good!"

Now let's take a moment to reflect on the 7th day:

There was anticipation that the creative acts of the Creator would again be purposed to reveal some new and grander creation but there was nothing: proving that God had ended and was finished with his creation, God ceased creating but he did not cease to be God.

God is the power of creation for by his will all that is known to man was created. The Sabbath was presented to Man in his perfect state, a window into eternity past, present and future. A perfect vantage point to view the mysteries of his Creator's omnipotence, omniscience, omnipresence and to recognize him as an all-loving Creator. The Sabbath is a reflection of Holiness, it is the mercy seat that exist in the presence of the most Holy.

The Sabbath permits us to admire and to acknowledge that God is the Alpha and the Omega the first and the Last, Holy, Righteous and Worthy of all honor and praise. After sin, the Sabbath continues to welcome man into God's Holy Presence for an experience of God's provision as a symbol of God's mercy and great love. And this is to be experienced at the conclusion of every week.

The Sabbath remains sanctified and set apart from the 6 days of the week to draw all Creation to comprehend God's intentional process to restore us. The Sabbath gathers us to come before our Creator to experience the greatest power of God which is God's Love. The Sabbath allows sinful man to observe the completeness and holiness of His Creator. It permits us to admire learn and to acknowledge that God is our Salvation. The Sabbath invites that experience.

Think about all of Creation known to man. Man was made in the image of God and was completed by the woman, crafted from a rib out of his side. Man was and is confronted with a greater mystery and a higher quest than he originally chose, to know his Creator. That knowledge and that experience should prevent us from straying.

Man is known more by his creator than he could know of his creator. But the week of Creation must be fully completed before creation is ended and after 6 Days the Man and the woman would agree with the pronouncement of their maker.

There is a saying that it's not over until it's over. God had created man for a noble purpose that suited him. God expressed a unique intent for man. Before God expressed his satisfaction with his creative expression, he outlined his high ideal for his crowning creation which was the Man and the woman. Certainly, we are special to God even though today, we are marred "damaged goods". He provided the Sabbath because he loved us from the beginning.

Let's review the creation account in scriptures verse by verse:

And God said, Let us make man in our image, after our likeness: and let them have dominion over the fish of the sea, and over the fowl of the air, and over the cattle, and over all the earth, and over every creeping thing that creepeth upon the earth. Genesis 1:26

So God created man in his own image, in the image of God created he him; male and female created he them. Genesis 1:27

And God blessed them, and God said unto them,

Be fruitful, and multiply, and replenish the earth, and subdue it: and have dominion over the fish of the sea, and over the fowl of the air, and over every living thing that moveth upon the earth. Genesis 1:28

And God said, Behold, I have given you every herb bearing seed, which is upon the face of all the earth, and every tree, in the which is the fruit of a tree yielding seed; to you it shall be for meat. Genesis 1:29

And to every beast of the earth, and to every fowl of the air, and to everything that creepeth upon the earth, wherein there is life, I have given every green herb for meat: and it was so. Genesis 1:30

Thus the heavens and the earth were finished, and all the host of them. Genesis 2:1

And on the seventh day God ended his work which he had made; and he rested on the seventh day from all his work which he had made. Genesis 2:2

And God blessed the seventh day, and sanctified it: because that in it he had rested from all his work which God created and made. Genesis 2:3

Remarkably the Sabbath is presented in such a way that even fallen man is forever linked to his Creator. As suggested previously and this must be emphasized: The Sabbath is a weekly reminder of a divine plan put in place that draws creation to reflect on its wonderful creator. It is a divine appointment with our maker.

For some it just commemorates God doing nothing and for those who are so careless not to see the truth or even investigate: evolutionism, agnosticism and atheism are the fruit of that ignorance. My Bible suggest that God determined to bless man. The Seventh day is set apart for man as a notable event, a day of sanctification and with sanctifying power. God did this for man by affixing the 6 days of Earths creation to it. The week is only complete with the 7th day.

Ironically Man was made on the 6th day and only completed by his wife and the breath of God in their lungs. So, man was not complete without the woman. The Week is begun with 6 days but not completed until God had established the Sabbath or linked the 6 days of Creation with the Sabbath which always was and always will be.

Christ was always God's offering for man. Our creator would always be our benefactor because everything that was made was made by him. Our care and provision reside in him. Christ was always ready to atone for man. God is Holy and Righteous, and we are His special creation.

"In the beginning was the Word, and the Word was with God, and the Word was God. He was with God in the beginning. Through him all things were made; without him nothing was made that has been made." John 1:1-3

The Sabbath is God's declaration of ownership of all creation. It is a Holy and a perfect expression of God's eternal love for his creation. The Sabbath is God's signature and seal, and mark of authenticity. Jesus Christ is Lord of the Sabbath; he is the proof of our promised redemption and in the Sabbath, he declares that we belong to him. Our fate was always in his loving hands.

"And it shall come to pass, *that* from one new moon to another, and from one sabbath to another, shall all flesh come to worship before me, saith the LORD." *Isaiah 66:23*

The Seventh Day Sabbath covenant that Israel was given was an acknowledgement that God was their God. Only by his mighty power, were they set free. The Bible says, *"Therefore the LORD your God commanded you to keep the Sabbath day."* *Deuteronomy 5:15*

In other words: That is why, or it was for that reason. If that was true for the Israelites, what does it mean for you and me today? The Sabbath is a good thing, it was always for our good.

CHAPTER 16

SET FREE

"But they and our fathers dealt proudly, and hardened their necks, and hearkened not to thy commandments, And refused to obey, neither were mindful of thy wonders that thou didst among them; but hardened their necks, and in their rebellion appointed a captain to return to their bondage: but thou art a God ready to pardon, gracious and merciful, slow to anger, and of great kindness, and forsookest them not." Nehemiah 9:16-17

Let's see what you know and understand. Were we or are we not Slaves in sin? Have not our bodies been chained and bound by sensuous desires due to our carnal nature? Have we not been forced into addictions and low acts of every kind and reminded that we will never be free? Has not the Devil been a cruel Slave master just as Pharaoh was towards Israel claiming them as property and undeserving of the right to worship their God? *Ref Exodus 10:7-11*

Have we not been denied access to the full liberating word of God substituted by false gods, false worship and altered faith? Did not God by his mighty power lift the curse of sins eternal claim on man, a claim which accuses us as unworthy and declares that we have no deliverance and no forgiveness? Are we not told that we are not righteous and that we cannot be Sons or Daughters of God?

Did not Jesus Christ die for the entire world so that whoever will choose to believe in Jesus Christ and the Eternal Love of the Father, can also and will also receive eternal life? Did not Christ promise rest for our souls? *Ref Matthew 11:29*

This remembrance, this conversion, this observance of the Sabbath is a demonstration of our faith, hope and love for God our creator and deliverer. The Sabbath experience that God invites us into is a foretaste of the future state of Glory that God promises in his word and thru his son Jesus Christ. More than that God is our father, and this gives us hope.

"The creation looks forward to the day when it will join God's children in glorious freedom from death and decay. For we know that all creation has been groaning as in the pains of childbirth right up to the present time. And we believers also groan, even though we have the Holy Spirit within us as a foretaste of future glory, for we long for our bodies to be released from sin and suffering. We, too, wait with eager hope for the day when God will give us our full rights as his adopted children, including the new bodies he has promised us." Romans 8:21-23 NLT

This same God who through a remnant of mankind out of one faithful man declared the birth of a holy nation of many people scattered and tattered, dispersed throughout the world. This God was faithful in providing deliverance for all mankind which is an even greater deliverance than that of Israel's deliverance from Egypt.

The Sabbath is a symbol of Godly rest and peace just as it was in the beginning when God ended creation and declared that it was good, and He rested. It is a sign that out of darkness and chaos the same God who created all things for his Glory, is worthy of all honor and worship. When man honors God, he is able to experience harmony with God and share in His Rest and experience the peace and joy of willful obedience without any burden or weight of guilt and sin.

God rested because his plan was perfect, and all provisions made. This is because God was prepared for every possible outcome when he gave man the power of choice. God gave man free will and the capacity to err and we do err consistently.

We love that freedom. We resist any hint of restriction even to this day. We settle into the notion that to err is human. We vehemently resist accountability and consequence. We were not created to be slaves. We were created to reason to think and to choose good over evil.

"Well then, since God's grace has set us free from the law, does that mean we can go on sinning? Of course not! Don't you realize that you become the slave of whatever you choose to obey? You can be a slave to sin, which leads to death, or you can

choose to obey God, which leads to righteous living." Rom 6:15-16 NLT

The Sabbath – God's Holy Rest is a covenant establishing a union between God and his faithful children. Those who desire to be called by His Name shall rest secure in the hope of Christ 2nd Advent and an endless day of rest from all earthly pain, suffering and sorrows.

The Sabbath is a sign and a reminder that God will put an end to his labors for mankind and an end to the labors of his obedient children. God will cause it all to cease, and he will one day declare it complete.

And then the judgment: Where God will finally cleanse the world of sin and that wall of separation will be removed forever. There will be a glorious and welcome reunion of God's redeemed. Those who will have freely chosen to obey him will be forever sealed, at rest and restored because they were reminded and took hope in his Salvation and never forgot their creator and savior again.

CHAPTER 17

A MARRIAGE

"And he saith unto me, Write, Blessed are they which are called unto the marriage supper of the Lamb. And he saith unto me, These are the true sayings of God." Revelations 19:9

The celebration of the Sabbath is not unlike the marriage union and covenant vow, till death do you part. The marriage's survival is marked by persistence within the union. The couple refuse to break the bonds. They honor the pledge and refuse to allow anyone to separate them pledging eternally to keep within its confines and maintain its sanctity, as long as they both shall live.

With the Sabbath, God has assured man that his promise is eternal as he is. He has secured our lives with the life of his Son Jesus Christ who offers us a refreshing and rest from the results of our failed promises. He offers this to all who are weary, heavy burdened and desiring to be united with him.

We should keep the Sabbath because we desire to honor the covenant. We are to keep it Holy because we honor God who is Holy. We remember that he is our Sabbath. Christ is our assurance, that united in his purpose we are made Holy by him. We should not take his name without reverence for it.

When God says "Remember the Sabbath Day": The Day of Promise, The Sign of His faithfulness and power, the seal of His Authenticity and Authority, what is God really saying? Remember me! We are in this together.

It is an invitation and an encouragement to all who desire to place their trust in him and place their lives under his authority to remember and never forget his promise. It is a covenant to persevere for our deliverance from sin.

"The kingdom of heaven is like a king who prepared a wedding banquet for his son. He sent his servants to those who had been invited to the banquet to tell them to come, but they refused to come. "Then he sent some more servants and said, 'Tell those who have been invited that I have prepared my dinner: My oxen and fattened cattle have been butchered, and everything is ready. Come to the wedding banquet." Mat 22:2-4 NIV

Can you see a parallel in this parable of a Marriage Celebration? A Banquet Feast has been prepared to invite honored guest to share in the union of the Kings Son with his princess bride. They refused and the King sends messengers to remind them to Save the Date, to RSVP to commit.

We who are easily offended, would take serious exception to those who were invited and declined the first time. We would hardly waste a second time after their obvious rejection. Why would we beg?

Now the King's invitation has his seal upon it reminding them that this is coming from the King and all the preparations have been made in advance. They knew of the pending nuptials long before they were to be invited. Finally all is ready and they are the invited guest of the Crowned Prince, his Son. On this special day they will not be required to provide anything but their presence. Wow this is seems so familiar. May God's Holy Spirit speak to you right now.

God's faithfulness throughout the scripture stands in contrast to our own unfaithfulness as he reminds us and reinvites us because of his great love and desire for us. There can be no better incentive to hold firm than to remember that the Lord of the Sabbath will provide deliverance and judgement.

We generally respond appropriately to the request of those we love. Where there has been a great benefit and generosity our response id generally to reciprocate and respond with loyalty.

God's people share God's grace when returning a faithful tithe and when blessing the Church and others with generous offerings. Accepting God's invitation is an offering of gratitude towards God when we worship and celebrate the Sabbath.

Why? because they are releasing the storehouse of God from captivity in their hands and pockets instead, they are sharing of His abundance, calling all who are so benefited to the same remembrance. They worship in such a way others will sense the goodness of their God.

To keep it holy... is to reverence it as consecrated to God and therefore sacred. The Scriptures maintain that it is a Holy day set apart by God and that God is worthy of worship and praise and obedience. It is God's everlasting covenant, just as the marriage covenant should be.

CHAPTER 18

NOT A THREAT

"Therefore, a time of rest and worship exists for God's people. Those who entered his place of rest also rested from their work as God did from his. So we must make every effort to enter that place of rest. Then no one will be lost by following the example of those who refused to obey. God's word is living and active. It is sharper than any two-edged sword and cuts as deep as the place where soul and spirit meet, the place where joints and marrow meet. God's word judges a person's thoughts and intentions. No creature can hide from God. Everything is uncovered and exposed for him to see. We must answer to him." Heb 4:9-13 GW

How do we learn to worship God and honor him in keeping the Sabbath holy? How do we understand the highly legalistic application of the Sabbath as a socially enforced behavior that carried a death sentence in Biblical times with a modern application that is not socially enforced? Those are great questions.

There is no way that I can endorse that historical and social ideology today. Something is wrong when we look back historically and take away the worst possible imagery and interpretation and we neglect the context and environment that was a catalyst to that historical behavior and world view.

Something is wrong when the promises of God for our good are ignored and our persistence in rebellion and sin finds justification in make God a villain. Are we not attempting to speak for God and interpret God's will without the context of our fallen state and undeniable consequences?

God's will is illustrated and revealed by his actions. It was also dictated to his prophets and prophetess and his ways demonstrated in all the stories found in the scriptures. While to us this method would seem flawed in the context of the almighty God communicating with man thru fallen men. There is no denying that with God's knowledge of our fragility and weakened state the urgency and methodology must bear a relatable significance.

So, these messenger's lives, and world views were also imprinted on the words of God. Their various perceptions and perspectives were certainly influenced by the times they lived in which also reflected their social interactions and expressions. These diverse influences were used to relate the things of God to their contemporaries at first but would also later be communicated to those of different eras.

Then I said, "It's all over! I am doomed, for I am a sinful man. I have filthy lips, and I live among a people with filthy lips. Yet I have seen the King, the LORD of Heaven's Armies." Isaiah 6:5 NLT

I am a Sabbatarian. I am not perfect in my practice of Sabbath observance as historically taught by Jews and other Sabbatarian followers including Seventh Day Adventist. The latter is the denomination that I was raised and baptized into and later rebaptized into because I believe that the word of God "the Bible" is God's communication to mankind. It is not of private interpretation and reveals God's relation to his creation throughout the scriptures.

The 10 Commandments begin with God declaring his authority and he makes his case in the 4th Commandment.

"And God spoke all these words, saying, I am the LORD your God, who brought you out of the land of Egypt, out of the house of slavery. You shall have no other gods before me.

You shall not make for yourself a carved image, or any likeness of anything that is in heaven above, or that is in the earth beneath, or that is in the water under the earth. You shall not bow down to them or serve them, for I the LORD your God am a jealous God, visiting the iniquity of the fathers on the children to the third and the fourth generation of those who hate me, but showing steadfast love to thousands of those who love me and keep my commandments.

You shall not take the name of the LORD your God in vain, for the LORD will not hold him guiltless who takes his name in vain.

Remember the Sabbath day, to keep it holy. Six days you shall labor, and do all your work, but the seventh day is a Sabbath to the LORD your God. On it you shall not do any work, you, or your son, or your daughter, your male servant, or your female servant, or your livestock, or the sojourner who is within your gates. For in six days the LORD made heaven and earth, the sea, and all that is in them, and rested on the seventh day. Therefore, the LORD blessed the Sabbath day and made it holy." Exodus 20:1-11 NIV

While some of this will certainly be brushed off as one man's opinion, I happen to believe that the study of the word of God with an earnest intent to gain knowledge and truth is rewarded with the comfort that God will provide us with what we seek if we seek with our full heart. The same confidence that Abraham spoke to Isaac saying that God will provide.

The state of society today is begging for a Sabbath. We need the Sabbath. Trying to observe it perfectly is a noble and needful aspiration, but we often forget that the Sabbath was set as a special day with purpose and significance that extend beyond our individual capacity.

The Sabbath has established parameters that expand beyond our scope of comprehension because it was purposed by God for our benefit. The solemnity of it is clear from the very beginning and there was no curse or negative context surrounding it, yet it was made for our good overriding our potential errors which have been realized ever since the forbidden fruit was touch and eaten.

CHAPTER 19

REST vs DEATH

"At that time Jesus answered and said, I thank thee, O Father, Lord of heaven and earth, because thou hast hid these things from the wise and prudent, and hast revealed them unto babes. Even so, Father: for so it seemed good in thy sight. All things are delivered unto me of my Father: and no man knoweth the Son, but the Father; neither knoweth any man the Father, save the Son, and he to whomsoever the Son will reveal him. Come unto me, all ye that labour and are heavy laden, and I will give you rest. Take my yoke upon you, and learn of me; for I am meek and lowly in heart: and ye shall find rest unto your souls." Matthew 11:25-29

These scriptures paint a picture of God's love and grace and Man's ineffectiveness to sustain holiness or to measure up. Even the fear of death could not perfect the souls and cleanse the hearts contaminated by sin.

"And the LORD spake unto Moses, saying, Speak thou also unto the children of Israel, saying, Verily my sabbaths ye shall keep: for it is a sign between me and you throughout your generations; that ye may know that I am the LORD that doth sanctify you. Ye shall keep the sabbath therefore; for it is holy unto you: every one that defileth it shall surely be put to death: for whosoever doeth any work therein, that soul shall be cut off from among his people.

Six days may work be done; but in the seventh is the sabbath of rest, holy to the LORD: whosoever doeth any work in the sabbath day, he shall surely be put to death. Wherefore the children of Israel shall keep the sabbath, to observe the sabbath throughout their generations, for a perpetual covenant. It is a sign between me and the children of Israel for ever: for in six days the LORD made heaven and earth, and on the seventh day he rested, and was refreshed. Exodus 31:12-17

Pronouncements of death over the Sabbath was more emblematic of the importance of the Sabbath and a declaration that God's faithful followers would never dishonor or break ranks by dishonoring the Sabbath any more than a Husband and Wife should desire to dishonor each other and break the marriage vows.

The common marriage covenant says till death do you part. What do we make of that? If the covenant is broken, do we take the life of the one who broke it today? Does the persistence of this vow today mean that our desire is to kill all cheaters and adulterers? I think not.

The fact is, no matter what the consequences are, sinful men and women have shown a persistence to defy and to hazard and risk all. Death is not a deterrent nor is it a prevention of sin. Death is a consequence of sin. More than that Death is the reward or wages of sin.

"For the wages of sin is death, but the free gift of God is eternal life through Christ Jesus our Lord."
Rom 6:23 NLT

Then said Jesus unto his disciples, If any man will come after me, let him deny himself, and take up his cross, and follow me. For whosoever will save his life shall lose it: and whosoever will lose his life for my sake shall find it. For what is a man profited, if he shall gain the whole world, and lose his own soul? or what shall a man give in exchange for his soul? For the Son of man shall come in the glory of his Father with his angels; and then he shall reward every man according to his works. Matthew 16:24-27

Jesus Christ our Savior and Sabbath has done what any legal standard cannot do. He has accepted our guilt and yet without sin persevered in a sinless life and guiltless death so that we can live not only in this world but in the new heaven and new earth to come.

The law does not save. Jesus saves! Our lives must be as submitted to Christ as he was committed to obeying his father. He laid down his life for our salvation and we should not expect to save our souls by disobeying him and pursuing our selfish desires in this world.

Again, the urgency of the matter, matters. How do you instruct the ignorant of the impending peril of perilous actions? How do you warn a child against dangerous and hazardous behavior?

Did not God warn Adam and Eve who did not know death that if they ate the forbidden fruit that they would die. Yet we are here today, and Adam and Eve dead. God did not sugar coat it and of course his servants the prophets and messengers understood well what the people would comprehend, relate to and respect.

97

Ultimately, for Israel to reject the God who delivered them was clearly a death sentence be it future or immediate. It was suicidal in today's context as willingly choosing death over life. They owed their existence to God who gave them the Sabbath. What other context might they have?

Egyptian slavery and culture that they grew up in was cruel and exacting. They were beaten and or killed for their failure or resistance. Their world view was tainted by their experience none the less they also understood that the Pharaoh did not have their good in mind.

I can only imagine that God's love and care shined very bright in their thoughts and his instructions and warnings were all the more meaningful even though tainted by their past. They understood that the Egyptian army was destroyed by God to protect them.

I imagine they were consumed with fear even to see their enemies drop like flies. Certainly, there was a fear of the consequence of failing and disappointing God. So, when they taught and expressed themselves, they were expressing God's instructions in the same terms as they could only comprehend or imagine.

Keep also in mind by the time the anticipated Messiah and Lord of the Sabbath was revealed they did not recognize him or comprehend his words and actions. They even accused him of being a Sabbath breaker and blasphemer, yet he was their Salvation, and he is ours as well.

CHAPTER 20

FAITH IN GOD

"You won't die!" the serpent replied to the woman. "God knows that your eyes will be opened as soon as you eat it, and you will be like God, knowing both good and evil." Gen 3:4-5 NLT

Don't be fooled. There will often be disagreements regarding faith's debating and even arguing the distinctions between them. This is only a natural manifestation in our sin ridden souls. We thrive on competition, and we challenge diversity wanting to receive affirmation as superior or on par with perfection. We want to be as God separating good from evil. Sound familiar?

There is in fact sound doctrine and there are in fact present truths but there are plenty of misapplications of truth. There is no Church or denomination that is unaffected by this.

Anyone who takes on the defiant task to go on the attack against the faith of a professed believer should have a clear sensitivity paired with accuracy to be applied first to themselves. They should use their tactics with surgical precision to their own faith, and belief system, just as they would apply to those of another's.

The truth reveals the real versus the counterfeit if it is applied in sincerity but all too often, we attempt to use a sledgehammer and a spike to separate a man or woman from their faith when refined water and a polishing cloth is all that is necessary for them to shine brighter and unbroken.

So, when we point out error or give counsel and direction, is our intent to show care and concern? Is it our desire to build up the individual or is it to shame, blame and degrade each other without mercy, humility or even an understanding for the reasons of their beliefs or present condition? The truth will be revealed.

Imagine taking a chisel to remove a splinter when a needle or pin might do. But even the correct tools should be sanitized, and it is best to use the most appropriate for extraction and safety of yourself and others. Witnessing for Christ requires a sensitive lens.

Love is always the lens of choice and a necessary motive. How else can we proceed without exposing ourselves to God's judgement and he is able to discern our hearts and motives, even to expose our inner demons and cherished pride and sin.

Jesus was clear that we need to check ourselves before we attempt to check and correct others.

"Why do you look at the speck of sawdust in your brother's eye and pay no attention to the plank in your own eye? How can you say to your brother, 'Let me take the speck out of your eye,' when all the time there is a plank in your own eye? You hypocrite, first take the plank out of your own eye, and then you will see clearly to remove the speck from your brother's eye." Matthew 7:3-5 NIV

Any defense of the Sabbath faith must start with God

and end with God and the believer. I must give an answer for the reason of my faith: If I fail to be honest, then I will have greatly disappointed God and veered from his Holy Word which is always the standard and ultimate authority. For anyone who is new to the Sabbath message, this should only be a starting point for you as it is for me.

"But sanctify the Lord God in your hearts: and be ready always to give an answer to every man that asketh you a reason of the hope that is in you with meekness and fear: Having a good conscience; that, whereas they speak evil of you, as of evildoers, they may be ashamed that falsely accuse your good conversation in Christ." 1Pe 3:15-16

The truth is, I can only reveal a slight glimpse of what God's word has shown me regarding the Sabbath, Christ and all humanity. This is my personal confession of faith and should be weighed as such. Before I began to write this book, I first asked myself what is so important about the Sabbath?

By now you already know the reason of my hope. The Sabbath affirms and anchor my hope. I hope you are challenged by my testimony but if you are also convicted to keep the Sabbath, I will take no credit. If you are convinced that it is not necessary then you alone must answer for your faith and the reason of your hope.

CHAPTER 21

A REASON FOR HOPE

So the LORD God said to the snake, "Because you have done this, You are cursed more than all the wild or domestic animals. You will crawl on your belly. You will be the lowest of animals as long as you live. I will make you and the woman hostile toward each other. I will make your descendants and her descendant hostile toward each other. He will crush your head, and you will bruise his heel."
Gen 3:14-15 GW

My hope causes me to believe that I am a Child of God, a beloved creation of God. Here on this earth which God created in the beginning to reveal his Triune Glory in the expression of his love, revealing himself to all his creation through his word and that expression of Love is the unifying power of God in human form which God promised to the then fallen Adam and Eve.

I believe that God's love was revealed and fulfilled in Jesus Christ. Jesus Christ was the promised conqueror of sin and death who would crush the head of the enemy and destroyer. The word of God, the Bible is God's testimony. It is the Testimony of Jesus Christ.

The word of God is the history of the origins of all things. The Bible chronicles the tragic fall of man and ultimately the History of man's salvation via prophetic revelations throughout it pages. The Sabbath was and is a prophetic sign of God's solidarity with his human creation man.

No matter who you think you are, you are here on earth and God is revealing himself to you thru his oral and written word which is evidenced in the visible physical and invisible realm. God is revealed in the past present and the future as our Creator and our only hope of Salvation.

As a result of sin, we are a marred and damaged creation that has not been abandoned as many will claim as they deny God. We have not evolved into a higher consciousness for the truth of God is revealed thru our persistent questions and inquiries regarding truth. God's truth is all around us. If we have open minds, we cannot ignore it.

The truth is, Evolution is a lie. If it were true, then we have no need to care for the circumstances of our current existence. If there was no design template or intent, why even fret? Why fear for our future?

We should have no need to attempt to craft or preserve or even imagine for a better future. Why look for a way to improve upon that which decays only and expect thing to somehow become better especially, when we have seen what is called progress today?

Zoos are still filled with Monkeys, Lizards, creeping and flying things and Aquariums are filled with aquatic life in all its various forms. Each reproducing after their kind. There is no Big Bang or Evolutionary theory that can begin to account for the eye let alone all of creation. The greatest mystery is that some have accepted the foolishness of man's efforts to explain his own existence.

If you are a believer, I could assume that evolution is not an adoption of your faith ideology. You may wonder how I have somehow averted the conversation of Sabbath keeping to a rebuttal of science while only concluding that like you that I am a creationist. Well, this will help you to understand the core of my thesis which you may find equally puzzling but bear with me.

Jesus Christ is for mankind and all of Creation, therefore Jesus Christ is represented by the Sabbath and becomes our constant hope that the Lord of the Sabbath will gather us together under his authority to commence in the keeping of the Sabbath. Sabbath keeping honors our creator and memorializes our Savior's task and sacrifice. This being my thesis serves as a basis for me to both keep the Sabbath, to study it and to seek to honor God in observing it as best I can.

Weather I worship a certain way or on a certain day should not be a defense for infallibility or justification of my personal faith. Nothing I do makes Christ the more real. There are many who claim to be believers and there are those who do not. While I do claim denominational affiliation, I do not claim that all its members including myself fully comprehend the breath and scope of eternal salvation.

I cannot affirm that every Seventh Day Adventist share the same inspiration or have the same revelation or would express the same belief regarding Sabbath significance only that God has presented enough evidence to them for them to respond affirmatively to the Sabbath.

I can only share what distinction of my faith facilitates my growth in Christ whether others claiming the same beliefs are faithful or not. Whether they are growing or not. I can only believe that they will find no fault in it. I am only concerned in God finding no fault in it.

You may say who am I to suggest who is faithful, growing or not? I say I am just a man and I live knowing that God must judge his servants individually just as he calls them to differing task and engages them to his work. It is his will they must satisfy and not mine.

"Who art thou that judgest another man's servant? to his own master he standeth or falleth. Yea, he shall be holden up: for God is able to make him stand." Romans 14:4

I have met truly Godly Christians where the Sabbath has not been the insatiable hole in their religious experience. This does not mean there is not a hole in their religious experience. Absence of the Sabbath creates that hole. Jesus Christ fills the hole in me. Christ spans the gap between our failings and his complete perfection.

Jesus Christ has authority and importance that he claims over the Sabbath. The same Sabbath which he honored and kept, he did so as an example according to the will of the father. In sanctifying the Sabbath to conclude creation, God established it as the ultimate benefit to man connecting man to God, extending God to man forever.

CHAPTER 22

GOD'S SIGNATURE

"And it shall come to pass, that from one new moon to another, and from one Sabbath to another, shall all flesh come to worship before me, saith the LORD." Isaiah 66:23

Sanctification is the setting apart for a holy purpose. Just as each day of the week was separated by evening and morning **Ref Genesis 1:5, 8, 13, 19, 23, 31** The SABBATH was further set apart by the creator for a Holy Purpose. **Ref Genesis 2:1-3.** This seminal act of uncreation ended the daily cycle and momentum of the creation week. At the same time its continuance appended to the creation cycle affirms the authenticity of original creation.

The setting of the sun on the fifth day precedes the beginnings of creation of man and the setting of the Sun on the sixth day affirms and demarks the end of that day of creation entirely. So the next day which would be the Seventh day, God simply created nothing. God distinguished it by this distinction:

"And on the seventh day God ended his work which he had made; and he rested on the seventh day from all his work which he had made. And God blessed the seventh day, and sanctified it because that in it he had rested from all his work which God created and made." Genesis 2:2-3.

The Sabbath reminds me that Creation was intentional

and purposeful and while man was a crowning creation of God on the 6th Day the presentation of the Sabbath was even more so significant as it was the climax of the Creator's expression sealing the connection between the Creator and His Creation much like the artist's finished rendering is sealed by the artist signature or imprint establishing its completion.

I am an artist. I draw. I often drew as a child and young man, and I never really liked doodling. I had intention in my art. I was not a cartoonist. I drew nature, animals and people. I desired realism and never perfected that. Humans were the hardest to draw because it was hard for me to capture the essence of them that made them uniquely individual.

I found that animals were easier because they were readily recognizable even if the model was not unique to me the goal and intent was always clear.

I have been asked why I don't draw much today and why I sort of stopped. It was because they never felt complete. I could never be satisfied that it was perfect or complete. I always wanted to tweak it or even start over. It just took too long, and I became frustrated. In fact, I did not always place my signature on a drawing because of that feeling of incompleteness.

God was not frustrated with his creation. God did not see it as incomplete. God knew the plans he had for his creation. God knew that it was very good, so he signed it with his signature, the Sabbath and sealed it.

"I know the plans that I have for you, declares the LORD. They are plans for peace and not disaster,

plans to give you a future filled with hope." Jeremiah 29:11GW

A forgery or missing signature would invalidate the work of any artist or creator as it would also taint the valuation and obscure the purpose and intent of the work of art. It would be incomplete no matter how wonderful or beautiful it may already appear if there were no signature.

Worship is the ultimate attribution of what we hold dearest and has primary focus in our lives. If we worship then we should worship God.

"Get out of here, Satan," Jesus told him. "For the Scriptures say, 'You must worship the LORD your God and serve only him." Matthew 4:10 NLT

How we worship should reflect an understanding of what pleases God. To understand that, we first have to know God. What we do know is God made the Sabbath Holy. If worship cannot begin in a holy space how can true worship begin at all?

How can we call it worship without first honoring that which God has made holy? If prayer is sacred and holy, then it is because it is to God. The Sabbath is holy and declared so by God who created all things.

A secret admirer may send a gift but without a revelation at some point that gift or gifts received cannot be fully appreciated or understood. It would seem purposeless or irrelevant. The Sabbath was made for man by whom? A gift from whom? For what purpose or benefit? A reasonable inquiry is necessary.

When you receive a meritless gift. Perhaps an unreasoning and ignorant person may not dare to consider its source. But we who call ourselves believers and lovers of God, as worshipers we would do well to consider and evaluate not only the gift but also the giver.

CHAPTER 23

TRUE WORSHIP

"But the time is coming—indeed it's here now—when true worshipers will worship the Father in spirit and in truth. The Father is looking for those who will worship him that way. For God is Spirit, so those who worship him must worship in spirit and in truth." John 4:23-24 NLT

I think it odd that every denomination including Non-Denomination have their own distinctions but there is only one God, one Christ and one Spirit. I believe there are truths that should be inter-denominationally held and affirmed by all believers in Jesus Christ. First and foremost, I believe that all should be believers in Jesus Christ and worship him.

I believe that there is only one name under heaven and earth that we can claim salvation through and that is Jesus Christ. There is unmistakably only one Sabbath. There are seven days in a week but only 1 day was set apart to mark the end of the week. The Seventh Day, the Sabbath.

So if everyone holds their own absolute views and they are affirmed by their own denominational entities then how is the Gospel appropriately spread and kept pure amid such diversity of men and women? Better yet in affirming my faith what doctrinal weight and denominational creed will I rely on in my profession of faith? How will I frame my answer? This quest and these questions predate the writing of the Bible. What can satisfy God? How can I maintain a healthy reverence for God?

"Will the LORD be pleased with thousands of rams or with endless streams of olive oil? Should I give him my firstborn child because of my rebellious acts? Should I give him my young child for my sin? You mortals, the LORD has told you what is good. This is what the LORD requires from you: to do what is right, to love mercy, and to live humbly with your God." Micah 6:7-8

The Bible is the word of God and Scriptures reflect the important things that God has chosen to communicate with us. Jesus Christ had this to say to the religious people of his day and in every age to follow, *"You search the Scriptures, because you think you will find eternal life in them. The Scriptures tell about me but you refuse to come to me for eternal life." John 5:39-40.*

I began this chapter referencing what Christ said to the Samaritan woman. For lack of a better word, she was of another denomination than the Jews. Here spiritual genealogy was of a mixed heritage and her beliefs were not considered compatible with Jewish beliefs.

I want to highlight Christ reference to God as the Father. Not just his father but hers. Not just the Father of Jews but the Father of Samaritans. He focused on the commonality of their combined interests, redirecting her to what the Father desires and not what we as individuals desire.

Since I believe that the Sabbath truth is proclaimed in

the scriptures then I must also believe that the Sabbath testifies about Jesus Christ, the Anointed and Sanctified Son of God. I believe that to not come to Christ and to refuse His significance is to be without hope or expectation.

The Sabbath gives me a hope and an expectation of eternal life as promised by the Creator of all things. So, I will embrace the Sabbath just as I am inspired to pray through a knowledge and acceptance of the Sabbath invitation.

By now you may have recognized or are familiar with my religious affiliation as a Seventh Day Adventist Christian. So, what can I say as a Seventh Day Adventist when I speak on the Sabbath? Is there any important point that I can share about my own affiliation?

I can say this, that as a Seventh Day Adventist, I am often at war an in constant debate within a body of believers some of whom have adopted a belief system that fails to unify the sexes and the cultures and falls helplessly in a cycle of purging and finger pointing which exposes personal unbelief and want and struggles to bear the burden that we place on them. So, in summary, we are not perfect.

Many members of my denomination believe we have the last day message and are on a path of God's remnant. Such a high calling requires greater humility and a servant's spirit. So, a self-reminder of the fact that Jesus is the Lord of the Sabbath is in order. I declare that I am affiliated with imperfect followers and believers of God and as one I admit without hesitation that I am imperfect and have often fallen short of my high calling

So besides our humanity exposed for the world to see I am not fearless to state that I believe all fellow believers as organizations struggle to live up to their own creed all being guilty of this common charge **"So you call yourself a Christian?!"** My religion is not unlike any other denominations including those united to declare that they are free of denominational ties.

Again, what can I say? In short what do I have that I can share with serious believers or defiant unbelievers? What should they consider of my writings and what do I write about? What should they consider of my conversation and what am I sharing? Only this:

1. I believe the Sabbath is a revelation of Jesus Christ. A ladder in the wilderness even Jacob's ladder *Ref Genesis 28:12.* A path that leads us from Slavery to triumph, from doubt to faith; from works to grace and from death to eternal life. I am writing for your prayerful consideration under divine inspiration that Jesus Christ is our Sabbath *Ref Mark 2:27-28.*

2. Christ is the beginning and the end of Man's creation. Christ is the eternal hope for all humanity and he alone is worthy of our obedience and praise for he calls us to repentance and offers us forgiveness of sin. He calls us from darkness and offers us freedom and light *Ref Luke 4:18-21.* He calls us from striving and labor to a burdenless yoke. *Ref Isa 58:6, 12-14, Ref Matt 11:29-30.* The Sabbath is a bridge and a yoke. The Sabbath provides and assures us of

God's rest, providing peace thru the salvation offered and promised by our Creator. This is the reason of my hope.

So this is the lens that I have centered to view the Sabbath through. It is the driving power that keeps me from totally giving up. Jesus Christ and him crucified for my sins and the whole world. Jesus Christ is my rest, and I am called to remember it.

The Bible is my text book and it is the word of Faith and chronicles of God: It is to disclose to all that God is real and there is Salvation thru faith in Jesus Christ the son of God! The Lord of the Sabbath.

Could I find some of this in any other Christian faith? Some, of course but the reason of the hope that is in me is found in the scriptures and hidden even in plain sight of many Seventh Day Adventist and other Sabbatarians. Jesus Christ is Lord of the Sabbath and that should turn our focus to his character and mission and actions towards the world, his followers and more significantly us.

While there are also earnest souls who believe in keeping the Sabbath on another day, they like the Samaritans neglect the precision of the word of God and they greatly miss what it is to honor God and worship God in spirit and in truth setting artificial boundaries to the service of God in favor of human reasoning and justification. This is also an error that I continue to struggle with.

CHAPTER 24

EYES ON THE PRIZE

"I don't mean to say that I have already achieved these things or that I have already reached perfection. But I press on to possess that perfection for which Christ Jesus first possessed me. No, dear brothers and sisters, I have not achieved it, but I focus on this one thing: Forgetting the past and looking forward to what lies ahead, I press on to reach the end of the race and receive the heavenly prize for which God, through Christ Jesus, is calling us. Let all who are spiritually mature agree on these things. If you disagree on some point, I believe God will make it plain to you. But we must hold on to the progress we have already made." Philipians 3:12-16 NLT

While I am would not deny the validity of the Sabbath. I often reason away or suppose that there is a work around doing what God requires. Our reasoning is not enough and should not trump the word of God.

Cain opened a door to sin and was warned when he offered a substitutionary sacrifice an offering of fruit, but no Lamb. What we are willing to offer to God reflects limitations of our understanding of what God wants to offer us. It is evidence of what holds the highest place in our hearts and minds. It also may reflect our personal fear of what God may be asking us to sacrifice.

The Sabbath is a weekly reminder that is set apart from the other six days. Each day brings us closer to the end of the week. Weekly we must be reminded that our daily labors can only satisfy our carnal needs. Each celebrated Sabbath brings us closer to the ultimate Sabbath in God presence. Each Sabbath awakens us to the reality that we are nothing without God.

Our accomplishments pale in comparison to what God has already done and they fall useless on the Sabbath day. Our daily toil and labors cannot influence or impress God or add to God. All our efforts must be set aside for the Glory and Honor of God. The Sabbath is an offer of Grace and Salvation that has been continually offered to the world. God is calling his creation to honor and worship him. *Ref Psalms 19:1-3*

I am reminded by a childhood song. "The B-I-B-L-E yes that's the book for me, I stand alone on the WORD OF GOD the B-I-B-L-E …" This is a song I have sung as a child and many children are still taught and sing it today. Its origins or author is not attributed but I do believe the lyrics of the song.

The Sabbath Rest, just as all the Bible, is wrapped up in Jesus Christ. Another Song accentuates this very fact. "The theme of the Bible is Jesus and how he died to save men, the plan of salvation assures us he's coming back again…Are you ready for Jesus to come? Are you faithful in all that you do? Have you fought a good fight have you stood for the right can others see Jesus in you… Are you ready for Jesus to come?" The Advent of Jesus Christ is heralded in this song [Are You Ready for Jesus to Come?] by Roy Pandleton.

The advent of Christ for most believers is both comforting and fearful as it heralds God's final judgement of the unbeliever and promises justification of the believer. The need for a savior at Christ second coming will have either been claimed or rejected when he appears. How confident are you that when he comes you will be found faithful?

Look! He comes with the clouds of heaven. And everyone will see him—even those who pierced him. And all the nations of the world will mourn for him. Yes! Amen! Revelations 1:7 NLT

Then everyone—the kings of the earth, the rulers, the generals, the wealthy, the powerful, and every slave and free person—all hid themselves in the caves and among the rocks of the mountains. And they cried to the mountains and the rocks, "Fall on us and hide us from the face of the one who sits on the throne and from the wrath of the Lamb. For the great day of their wrath has come, and who is able to survive?" Revelations 6:15-17 NLT

And then shall that Wicked be revealed, whom the Lord shall consume with the spirit of his mouth, and shall destroy with the brightness of his coming: 2 Thessalonians 2:8

Can we see ourselves at the end of each week come before our Lord and Savior the Creator of all things and the owner of the breath that is in our lungs? Are we not humbled as we bring our tithes, offerings, and accomplishments or share our talents in His presence?

What an unbearable burden it is to try to earn salvation and compare our sacrifice to the incomparable sacrifice of God because of his love for the world. *Ref John 3:16*

There is a time and place that God has set aside for us to come before him and to worship. To find healing, rest and relief. There is a day that God reminds us of, and it stands as an open invitation for us to seek relief and enter into Godly Rest and experience it as God intended and desires us to. The greatest error of believers is the thought that we can somehow earn Salvation which was secured by the blood of the Son of God.

Our sinful souls need rest and cleansing. Our lives need repurposing. The longing of our being must be turned to God. Our only escape from these bodies of sin is to cast our burden of sin at the foot of the Cross.

Remember our creator, repent and be reborn. The ignorance of the past is ignored but God is calling us to come to the light. We are to seek truth and dig a little deeper for it if necessary. We are to elevate our minds and lift our gaze a little higher and keep our eyes on the prize.

CHAPTER 25

EMBRACE THE LIGHT

"For everyone that doeth evil hateth the light, neither cometh to the light, lest his deeds should be reproved. But he that doeth truth cometh to the light, that his deeds may be made manifest, that they are wrought in God." John 3:20-21.

By now there are many who are wrestling with this new revelation or way of looking at the Sabbath and Jesus Christ declaration. This becomes light for you, and it is illuminating a glaring void in your knowledge of God's will for you. This can awaken a great transformation for you which can be a tremendous experience in your relationship with God.

Paul is a chief example of a transformation that is worthy of recognition. Paul reflects humility and true repentance. His actions turned from darkness and hatred to love and light which was evidenced by his works after accepting the call and mission of Christ.

"I thank Christ Jesus our Lord, who has given me strength to do his work. He considered me trustworthy and appointed me to serve him, even though I used to blaspheme the name of Christ. In my insolence, I persecuted his people. But God had mercy on me because I did it in ignorance and unbelief.

Oh, how generous and gracious our Lord was! He

filled me with the faith and love that come from Christ Jesus. This is a trustworthy saying, and everyone should accept it: "Christ Jesus came into the world to save sinners"—and I am the worst of them all.

But God had mercy on me so that Christ Jesus could use me as a prime example of his great patience with even the worst sinners. Then others will realize that they, too, can believe in him and receive eternal life. All honor and glory to God forever and ever! He is the eternal King, the unseen one who never dies; he alone is God. Amen." 1 Timothy 1:12-17 NLT

All of the scripture were designed to help us see the Love of God the Father who gave us the Son, Jesus Christ. His faithfulness, revealed to us the love of God and the Holy Spirit who empowers us to understand the word of God and live with Christ in us. I find this to be true in the study of the 7th Day Sabbath. While our differences often define us, our character is what is remembered about us. God's benevolent Character is memorialized in the Sabbath. He that has an ear to hear let him hear.

Today the world is in a riotous cry wanting to crucify God the Father afresh because they are ignorant. They say, "God is Dead!" they challenge God's power and sovereignty. Believing God impotent because he has permitted sin and suffering. Yet they do not repent of their sins.

Many deny God's authority by the overwhelming evidence presented by the character of many so-called believers of which I no doubt have had a share in. They are incredulous to the claims of God's Love and Holiness in the face of a profane society that is indifferent to the suffering of the innocent.

The proliferation of war, greed-based violence, abuse, indiscriminate tragedies in nature, including disease, suffering, hunger, poverty, and death. So, they deny God as creator or as having any authority in their lives.

What hope do believers have to offer the world? Additionally, how can true believers also ignore God's authority as the creator and not try to honor and worship him as he ordained?

The Sabbath becomes a weekly memorial of our hope in Christ for our reunion with the father. Shouldn't we desire to be transformed and made new? Shouldn't we desire to return into God's presence weekly? Shouldn't we desire to enter his presence with our heads held high because we are his children and belong?

"But as many as received him, to them gave he power to become the sons of God, even to them that believe on his name: Which were born, not of blood, nor of the will of the flesh, nor of the will of man, but of God." John 1:12-13.

You may say I know and honor God as creator and the author of salvation and declare this to be your faith, but our actions should reflect that reverence if we understand and desire to do what is most pleasing to

God. The Sabbath embodies the Love of God for mankind.

We ought to honor the Sabbath and demonstrate God's love to others. The many good and right things that we believe and do show a portion of faith in our words and deeds, also conspire to condemn us for what we do not do. So, it is not just Sabbath observance that should be part of our transformation.

"How horrible it will be for you Pharisees! You give God one-tenth of your mint, spices, and every garden herb. But you have ignored justice and the love of God. You should have done these things without ignoring the others." Luke 11:42

To obey, honor and respect any of the 10 commandments because it is of God, accentuates our honor and respect of the remaining. To accept the first 3 Commandments implies there would be agreement with the Sabbath Commandment which affirms God's authority over the lives of men and women and all creation.

Fidelity to God who instructs us beyond the 4th commandment on how we should live with our fellow man beginning with the 5th which calls us to honor our parents before we even begin to interact with others is telling. If God is your father, you cannot fail to see the significance.

Some of the commandments are easier to keep because of the fear of consequence from man. Believers must also have a conscience towards God. His authority, His name, His image, Deity and Power which allows us to come into harmony with God and restore order to our fallen nature.

It is no small thing to ignore the 4th Commandment because of its foundational and fundamental connection with our behaviors, philosophies and social interactions. The Sabbath is a reminder to remember whose we are and where we come from. It is also a reminder that we are marred. We are God's creation. So, who can fix us but God? The Sabbath reminds us of who God is. Christ is our Sabbath! He is our creator and like a potter, he alone can restore us.

"And the vessel that he made of clay was marred in the hand of the potter: so he made it again another vessel, as seemed good to the potter to make it. Then the word of the LORD came to me, saying, O house of Israel, cannot I do with you as this potter? saith the LORD. Behold, as the clay is in the potter's hand, so are ye in mine hand, O house of Israel. Jeremiah 18:4-6

Perhaps by now you are very concerned and uncomfortable with the thrust of my defense of Sabbath observance, but it is not I who can convict or change you. It is the Divine Holy Spirit that is opening your conscience toward the Sabbath Truth.

Most objections to the Sabbath involve the fear of its restrictiveness to our personal freedoms. We want to do what we want to do and when we want to do it. Like

Cain we are exposed not by what we profess but what we do and neglect to do. Only the word of God can separate us from our cherished beliefs and traditions.

CHAPTER 26

RE-INVITED

"For the word of God is quick, and powerful, and sharper than any two-edged sword, piercing even to the dividing asunder of soul and spirit, and of the joints and marrow, and is a discerner of the thoughts and intents of the heart." Hebrews 12:4

If the Sabbath Commandment knits us to God, it becomes our invitation to know, to worship and seek salvation from our Creator. How can we turn our backs on that? Ignorance and confusion are temporary constraints are good hiding places for those who desire avoid obedience.

How can we as Children of God jump on the furniture in His house? Think about it. Instead, we would discourage others from doing that. We would show them how to show respect to God. How to treat his home. We would certainly demonstrate by our actions, and we would know that he would be pleased by our devotion.

This is the reason of the hope that is within me. Jesus Christ in all of the Scripture compels me and he invites you to reason, study and to accept his invitation. I pray that you will.

"Study to shew thyself approved unto God, a workman that needeth not to be ashamed, rightly dividing the word of truth." 2 Timothy 2:15

We can believe anything and whether we were born into our belief or not. we an ability to study, to comprehend and to be guided by the spirit of God. There is tradition or superstition and there is the truth. We should not follow the commandments of men. These are traditions that deviate from God's word.

"Ye hypocrites, well did Esaias prophesy of you, saying, This people draweth nigh unto me with their mouth, and honoureth me with their lips; but their heart is far from me. But in vain they do worship me, teaching for doctrines the commandments of men." Mat 15:7-9

"Not giving heed to Jewish fables, and commandments of men, that turn from the truth. Unto the pure all things are pure: but unto them that are defiled and unbelieving is nothing pure; but even their mind and conscience is defiled. They profess that they know God; but in works they deny him, being abominable, and disobedient, and unto every good work reprobate." Tit 1:14-16

"Behold, the days are coming, declares the LORD, when I will make a new covenant with the house of Israel and the house of Judah, not like the covenant that I made with their fathers on the day when I took them by the hand to bring them out of the land of Egypt, my covenant that they broke, though I was their husband, declares the LORD.

For this is the covenant that I will make with the house of Israel after those days, declares the LORD: I will put my law within them, and I will write it on their hearts. And I will be their God, and they shall be my people.

And no longer shall each one teach his neighbor and each his brother, saying, 'Know the LORD,' for they shall all know me, from the least of them to the greatest, declares the LORD. For I will forgive their iniquity, and I will remember their sin no more." *Jeremiah 33:31-34 ESV*

The Lord is working on me to convert my heart and to bring me into agreement with him. My prayer is that you prayerfully consider this message and invitation about the Sabbath. May you be humble and teachable. For God loves you and this is a truth that can be the beginning of a richer experience and knowledge of God. My prayer is that you will glorify him and spread his love to all you meet.

"And if it seem evil unto you to serve the LORD, choose you this day whom ye will serve; whether the gods which your fathers served that were on the other side of the flood, or the gods of the Amorites, in whose land ye dwell: but as for me and my house, we will serve the LORD." Joshua 24:15

May God richly bless you as you contemplate this message and what it means to you. God wants to fill your life with hope. God wants to spend eternity with you. If that is your hope you will want to accept his invitation. If you had received it and set it aside you no longer need to look any further, you are re-invited.

WHAT IS THE SABBATH?

The Sabbath is "Resting with God".
Sabbath rest is not meditation or passive reflection or a nap time.
it is a full surrender of the will by a man or woman to God.
It is the exhale of the passions and desires of a human soul into
the confidence of our Loving Creator for renewal and refreshing.
It is waiting on the Lord who created the soul.
It is the inhale of the Grace of God's promises and life affirming
faith.
It is closing our eyes to the world around us and opening them to
the beauty of holiness, wholeness, freedom and release from our
daily burdens and sin.
The Sabbath is Holy,
it is the primary and preferred place of habitation for the believer
in God as creator.
The Sabbath is where the sinful and the righteous are openly
invited to come into a secure place and be reclaimed and restored
in harmony with the will of the Creator of Life. The will of a
triune God. The trinity known as God the father, God the Son
Jesus Christ and God the Holy Ghost.
The Sabbath is a sacred provision that provides for our needs and
promises that our prayers are heard and promises that our hopes
are well founded and that we can have true fellowship with God.
The Sabbath is a reminder of all of this, and we must remember
its significance. We should be encouraged by it.
So, if that sounds good, we should not reject it and instead we
can begin to discuss a distinction that is available for all to
acknowledge. The Sabbath is not faith, and it is not a practice or
belief it is the arena where our faith can truly be satisfied.

You have been formally re-invited to experience it.

THE LORD OF THE SABBATH

Invites You to Save the Date

And the angel said to me, "Write this: Blessed are those who are invited to the wedding feast of the Lamb." And he added, "These are true words that come from God." Revelations 19:9 NLT

Amen